Practice Tests Plus Volume 1

C1 Advanced

NEW EDITION

TEACHING
NOT JUST TESTING

Pearson Education Limited

KAO Two
KAO Park
Harlow
Essex CM17 9NA
England
and Associated Companies throughout the world.

www.pearsonELT.com

© Pearson Education Limited 2018

The right of Nick Kenny and Jacky Newbrook to be identified as authors of this Work has been asserted by them in accordance with the Copyright, Designs and Patents Act 1988.

All rights reserved; no part of this publication may be reproduced, stored in a retrieval system, or transmitted in any form or by any means, electronic, mechanical, photocopying, recording, or otherwise without the prior written permission of the Publishers.

First published 2018

ISBN: 978-1-292-20871-8
Set in Helvetica Neue LT 10/11.5pt and Gill Sans 8.5/10pt

Acknowledgements

With thanks to teachers and students from Eurocentres for providing sample student answers.

Billie Jago for providing sample student answers.

The publisher would like to thank the following for their kind permission to reproduce their texts:

Page 8 From the Financial Times 25 June 2005 "On a wing and a woof by Michael Cassell" © The Financial Times Limited 2005. All Rights Reserved; Page 10 "Whiff of Legend" by Kate Shapland © Telegraph Media Group Limited, 2007; "A boy named Nancy" by Chris Ayres, Saturday Times Magazine, 31 July 2004 © www.timeincukcontent.com; Page 14 From the Financial Times 23 September 2016 "Mind your language the fightback against global English" by Michael Skapinker. © The Financial Times Limited 2016. All Rights Reserved; Page 17 "Cornwall's Surfers up in arms at plans to harvest wave energy" by Michael McCarthy, The Independent, 28 April 2007; Page 24 "Interview with Eddie Irvine" by Nick Wyke, Saturday Times Magazine, 6th July 2002. Used with permission of The News Syndication; Page 25 "Could you write our winning short story" Woman & Home, May 2007 © www.timeincukcontent.com; Page 26 "Pime Tips" by Michael Brown, TNT Magazine, 15 September 2003, edition 1046 copyright www.tntmagazine.com; Page 27, 108 "Who's Listening?" by Helen Brown, The Independent, 4 May 2007; Page 32 From "The Long Way Round" by Ewan McGregor and Charley Boorman Copyright © 2004 by Time Warner Books (Little, Brown book group); Page 34 "Model Citizen" by Sabine Dupont, The Stella Magazine, 03 June 2007 © Telegraph Media Group Limited, 2007; Page 40 "Pigeon texters" by metrowebukmetro, Metro, 2 Feb 2006, Used with permission of The Associated Newspapers Ltd; From the Financial Times 12 March 2017 "College Tutors" by John Gapper © The Financial Times Limited 2017. All Rights Reserved; Page 41 From the Financial Time 29 November 2003 "Bags of confidence" by Damian Foxe © The Financial Times Limited 2003. All Rights Reserved; Page 42 "Forget Niagara" by Natasha Loder, Economist Intelligent Lift Summer 2006. Used with permission of The Economist Newspaper Ltd; Page 49 "Embracing the Office Revolution" by Ben Rooney © Telegraph Media Group Limited 2003; Page 56 "The Role of the Presenter" by Richard Mabey both, BBC Wildlife, May 2007. Used with permission of The BBC Wildlife; Page 58 "The new big brother" by Simon Davies © Telegraph Media Group Limited, 2003; Page 64 "War on Tat" by Adam Nicolson © Telegraph Media Group Limited, 2007; Page 65 "Kazutoshi Endo" by Hannah Duguid, The Independent Supplement Poise Magazine, 23 June 2007. Use with permission of The Independent; Page 74 Cambridgeshire Evening News for an extract adapted from "Leading the Field" by Chris Elliott published in Cabridgeshire Journal 1 February 2006; Page 80 From the Financial Time 04 May 2007 "Stiff breeze, no cocktails" by Victor Mallet. © The Financial Times Limited 2007. All Rights Reserved; Page 82 'Excerpt(s) from "Saturday" by Ian McEwan published by Jonathan Cape, 2005, an imprint of Penguin Publishing Group, a division of Penguin Random House LLC. All rights reserved; Page 85 'From the Financial Time 23 June 2007 "Gullible's travels" by Susan Elderkin. © The Financial Times Limited 2007. All Rights Reserved; Page 88 "Games People Play" by Sue Corbett, Sunday Express Magazine 23 April 2000. Used with permission of Sunday Express; Page 90 "Speed Read" by Milly Jenknis, Evening Standard, 26 November 2001.Used with permission of The Independent; Page 95 "The Show goes on for a Circus Double Act" by John, The Times Crème, 28 February 2000. Used with permission of The News Syndication; Page 106 Used with permission of The EasyJet Magazine, ©Ink; From the Financial Time 28 January 2016 "Michael Pawlyn, the architect inspired by nature" by John Thornhill. © The Financial Times Limited 2016. All Rights Reserved; Page 114 "Real men wash dishes" by Jemma Lewis © Telegraph Media Group Limited, 2003; Page 128 "Why Susannah swapped law for literature" East Anglian Times, 26 Feb 2010. Used with permission of The Archant Community Media Ltd; Page 132 The New Home Office by Oliver Heath" Move or Improve Magazine, May 2007. Used with permission of The Centaur Special Interest Media 2007; Page 133 From the Financial Time 01 April 2007 "Gorge yourself" by Simon de Burton. © The Financial Times Limited 2007. All Rights Reserved; Page 136 "Madness of the Safety Czars" by Simon Jenkins, The Evening Standard, 24 July 2003. Used with permission of The Independent; Page 140 From the Financial Time 04 August 2007 "Hidden depths" by Clive Cookson. © The Financial Times Limited 2007. All Rights Reserved; Page 142 "The man who invented a golden egg" by Guy Adams, The Independent, 23 June 2007; Page 146 "Don't fear the beaver" by Gail Vines © 2007 New Scientist Ltd. All rights reserved. Distributed by Tribune Content Agency.

The publisher would like to thank the following for their kind permission to reproduce their photographs:

(Key: b-bottom; c-centre; l-left; r-right; t-top)

123RF.com: 185b, Jean-Marie Guyon 185c, Zoran Jagrovic 180c, kzenon 174t, Tyler Olson 170b, 189t, sjenner13 178c, Igor Zhuravlov 180b; **Alamy Stock Photo:** aia image 188c, Bill Bachman 186c, CTK 173c, EmmePi Travel 186t, Tim Graham 179b, Hero Images Inc. 170c, 172b, Eddie Linssen 172c, Derek Meijer 174b, Roger Parkes 179c, Ted Pink 179t, Radius Images 184t, Geoff Smith 178t, Gregg Vignal 184b, Valery Voennyy 176c, Wavebreak Media ltd 173b; **Getty Images:** Dirk Anschutz 186b, Martin Harvey 182c, Jason Hetherington 170t, RPM Pictures 176b, sturti 189c; **Shutterstock.com:** BlueOrange Studio 182t, Raphael Daniaud 178b, Ditty_about_summer 172t, Greg Epperson 180t, Sergey Furtaev 188b, Helioscribe 174c, Denis Makarenko 176t, Monkey Business Images 173t, Tyler Olson 188t, pirita 182b, Pressmaster 185t, Vintagepix 184c, wavebreakmedia 189b

All other images © Pearson Education

Every effort has been made to trace the copyright holders and we apologise in advance for any unintentional omissions. We would be pleased to insert the appropriate acknowledgement in any subsequent edition of this publication.

CONTENTS

Exam Overview	4
Practice Test 1	**6**
Reading and Use of English	6
Writing	20
Listening	23
Speaking	29
Practice Test 2	**32**
Reading and Use of English	32
Writing	46
Listening	49
Speaking	55
Practice Test 3	**58**
Reading and Use of English	58
Writing	70
Listening	72
Speaking	77
Practice Test 4	**78**
Reading and Use of English	78
Writing	90
Listening	92
Speaking	97
Practice Test 5	**98**
Reading and Use of English	98
Writing	110
Listening	112
Speaking	117

Practice Test 6	**118**
Reading and Use of English	118
Writing	130
Listening	132
Speaking	137
Practice Test 7	**138**
Reading and Use of English	138
Writing	150
Listening	152
Speaking	157
Speaking Bank	**158**
Writing Bank	**163**
Visuals Bank	**170**
Test 1	170
Test 2	173
Test 3	176
Test 4	179
Test 5	182
Test 6	185
Test 7	188

EXAM OVERVIEW

The **Cambridge English Qualification C1 Advanced Exam**, also known as the **Cambridge Advanced,** is set at C1 Level on the Common European Framework of Reference scale. Cambridge Advanced offers a high-level qualification to people wanting to use their English for professional or study purposes. It consists of four papers: the Reading and Use of English paper carries 40 percent of the marks and the other three papers each carry 20 percent of the marks.

Reading and Use of English	1 hour 30 minutes
Writing	1 hour 30 minutes
Listening	40 minutes (approximately)
Speaking	15 minutes for each pair of students (approximately)

All the examination questions are task-based and stimulate real-life tasks. Rubrics (instructions) are important and should be read carefully. They set the context and give important information about the tasks. There is a separate answer sheet for recording answers for the Reading and Use of English and Listening papers.

Paper	Formats	Task focus
Reading and Use of English eight parts 56 questions	**Part 1:** short text with a multiple-choice cloze task	**Part 1:** use of vocabulary, e.g. idioms, collocations, fixed phrases, complementation, phrasal verbs
	Part 2: short text with an open cloze task	**Part 2:** sentence structure and accurate use of grammar
	Part 3: short text with a word formation cloze task	**Part 3:** use of the correct form of a given word in context
	Part 4: key word transformations	**Part 4:** use of grammatical and lexical structures
	Part 5: one long text with six multiple-choice questions	**Part 5:** reading for detailed understanding of a text, including opinion, attitude, tone, purpose, main ideas
	Part 6: four short texts with four multiple-matching questions	**Part 6:** comparing and contrasting opinions and attitudes across different texts
	Part 7: one long text with a gapped-paragraphs task (choosing which paragraphs fit into gaps in a base text)	**Part 7:** reading to understand text structure, coherence and cohesion
	Part 8: one long text divided into sections, or a series of short texts, with a multiple-matching task	**Part 8:** reading to locate relevant ideas and information in a text or texts
Writing **Part 1:** one compulsory task	**Part 1:** input texts provide the context and content for an essay of 220–260 words	**Part 1:** producing an essay based on two points given in the input text. Candidates have to evaluate the points and express their own opinions, giving reasons
Part 2: one task from a choice of three	**Part 2:** instructions give information about context, text type, target reader and purpose of a text of 220–260 words	**Part 2:** writing for a specific reader using appropriate layout and register. Possible genres are: letter, proposal, report and review

Paper	Formats	Task focus
Listening four tasks 30 questions	**Part 1:** three short unrelated extracts with two multiple-choice questions on each	**Part 1:** understanding gist, feeling, attitude, opinion, speaker purpose, etc.
	Part 2: long text with a sentence-completion task	**Part 2:** locating and recording specific information
	Part 3: long text with multiple-choice questions	**Part 3:** understanding attitude and opinion
	Part 4: series of five monologues on a theme with a multiple-matching task	**Part 4:** understanding gist, attitude, main points, etc.
Speaking four tasks	**Part 1:** a short conversation	**Part 1:** general interactional and social language
	Part 2: individual long turn based on visual prompts	**Part 2:** comparing and speculating
	Part 3: two-way conversation between candidates based on a question and written prompts	**Part 3:** giving and eliciting opinion, negotiating, turn-taking, etc.
	Part 4: discussion on topics related to Part 3	**Part 4:** expressing and justifying opinions and ideas

GUIDANCE: READING AND USE OF ENGLISH

PARTS 1-4

About the paper

The Reading and Use of English paper lasts for one hour and 30 minutes. There are eight parts to the paper, and a total of 56 questions. You have to read texts of different types and different lengths, for example, extracts from newspapers, magazines, websites and novels, as well as other short texts.

Part 1
You read a short text and answer eight multiple-choice questions. There are eight gaps in the text and you have to choose the word or phrase from a choice of four which fits best in each gap.

Part 2
You read a short text and answer open-cloze questions. There are eight gaps in the text. You have to fill each gap with the missing word.

Part 3
You read a short text and answer eight word-formation questions. There are eight gaps in the text and you're given the base form of the missing word. You have to change each word into the form in which it makes sense in the gap.

Part 4
You read six pairs of sentences and answer key word transformation questions. The pairs of sentences have the same meaning, but are expressed in different ways. There's a gap in the second sentence, which you have to fill with between three and six words. You're given one of these words. The key word must not change in any way.

How to do the paper

Part 1
- Read the text, ignoring the gaps, to get a general understanding.
- Only one of the options (A–D) fits the gap.
- Check the words before and after the gap. For example, some words can only be followed by one preposition, or may form part of a common collocation.
- Some questions focus on linking words, and you may need to understand the meaning of the whole text to know which word is correct in the context.
- If you're not sure which word to choose, go through the options and eliminate the answers you know are wrong.
- When you've finished, read the whole text again and check that it makes full sense with your answers in the gaps.

Part 2
- Read the text, ignoring the gaps, to get a general understanding.
- Think about the missing words. You only need to put one word in each gap and it's usually a grammatical word, e.g. a pronoun, linker or preposition.
- Before you fill each gap, read the sentence carefully and think about the type of word that's missing. For example, it may be linking two ideas, or part of a fixed phrase.
- When you've finished, read the whole text again and check that it makes full sense with your answers in the gaps.

Part 3
- Read the text, ignoring the gaps, to get a general understanding.
- Think about the missing words. You only need to put one word in each gap, and the base form of that word is written in capital letters at the end of the line.
- Before you fill each gap, read the sentence carefully and think about the type of word that's missing. For example, is it a noun, an adjective, an adverb?
- Change the word you've been given so that it fits the gap. You may need to add a prefix and a suffix or make other changes.
- Check whether nouns need to be singular or plural.
- Check that you've spelled the new word correctly.

Part 4
- Read the first sentence carefully to make sure you understand exactly what it means.
- Look at the key word. What type of word is it? What usually follows it. For example, is it an infinitive, a preposition, or could it be part of a fixed phrase or phrasal verb?
- The second sentence has the same information as the first sentence, expressed in a different order. Think about how the words need to change in the new order. For example, an adjective may become a noun or vice versa.
- You can include words and phrases in your answer that aren't used in the first sentence, as long as the meaning is the same.
- Check that your answer has between three and six words. Remember that contracted words count as two words, e.g. *won't = will not*.
- Check that the two sentences have exactly the same meaning with your answer in the gap.

PARTS 5-8
READING AND USE OF ENGLISH

About the paper

Part 5
You read a long text and answer six multiple-choice questions. There are four options in each question and the questions follow the order of information in the text.

Part 6
You read four short texts on the same topic. There are four questions which report the views and opinions of the different writers of the four texts. You have to match each question to the correct text or the correct writer.

Part 7
You read one long text from which six paragraphs have been removed. These paragraphs are placed in a jumbled order after the text, together with a seventh paragraph that doesn't fit in any of the gaps. You have to use your knowledge of grammar, vocabulary and referencing to work out which paragraph goes in each gap.

Part 8
You read either a long text divided into sections, or a series of short texts on the same topic. There are ten questions which report information and ideas from the text(s). You have to match each question to the correct section in the text.

How to do the paper

Part 5
- Read the text quickly to get a general understanding of what it's about and how it's organised.
- Read through the questions or question stems without looking at the options (A–D) and underline key words.
- Find the section of text where the question is answered and read it carefully, underlining key words and phrases.
- Try to answer the question in your own mind. Then look at options A–D and choose the one that's closest to your own answer. Look for the same ideas expressed in different ways.
- Check that the other options are definitely wrong. If you're still not completely sure, go through and work out why the other options are wrong.

Part 6
- Read the questions (37–40) first, underlining key words and ideas. There are two main types of question. In most questions you're told which section of text to read and which ideas you're looking for. Do these questions first and follow this process.
  - Read the section of text mentioned in the question and find the relevant topic or idea. Read this carefully to make sure you understand what the writer thinks about it.
  - The question then asks you to compare the writer's ideas on the topic with those of the other three writers. You may have to decide who has the same ideas and opinions, or who expresses different ones.
  - Now read the other texts carefully to find references to the topic or idea. Then read these sections carefully to make sure you've found the writer who has the same or different ideas.
- In the other type of question, you're told the topic or idea and asked to find the writer who has a different opinion to the others on that topic first and follow this process.
  - Read all the texts to find references to the topic or idea mentioned in the question.
  - Read the sections carefully to see which writer has different ideas to the other three on this topic.

Part 7
- Read the base text first, ignoring the gaps, to get a general idea of what it's about and how it's organised.
- Next, read the text around each gap carefully and think about the type of information which might be in the missing paragraph.
- Read paragraphs A–G. Check for topic and language links with the base text. Highlight words that relate to people, places and events, plus any time references. This will help you to follow the development of the argument or narrative.
- Choose the best option to fit each gap. Make sure that all the pronoun and vocabulary references are clear.
- Once you've finished, re-read the complete text to be sure that it makes sense with your answers in the gaps.

Part 8
- You don't need to read the whole text or set of texts first. That's why the questions are written before the text.
- Begin by reading questions 47–56 first, underlining the key words and ideas.
- Then read through the text(s) quickly and find information or ideas that are relevant to each question.
- For each question, when you find the relevant piece of text, read it very carefully to make sure that it completely matches the meaning of the question.
- You'll probably find references to the ideas in the question in more than one section of the text, but only one section exactly matches the idea in the question. You need to read all these sections carefully to find the exact match.

Part 1

For questions **1 – 8**, read the text below and decide which answer (**A, B, C** or **D**) best fits each gap. There is an example at the beginning (**0**).

In the exam, you mark your answers **on a separate answer sheet**.

Example:
0   **A** allows   **B** makes   **C** lets   **D** means

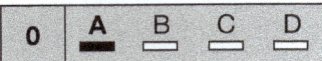

The Wave Hub

The Wave Hub is a giant electrical terminal located on the seabed ten miles off the coast of Cornwall in southwest England. It **(0)** .... a number of different wave-energy devices operating in the area to transmit the energy they generate along a high-voltage undersea cable, back to the shore.

When it first **(1)** .... into operation, the Wave Hub marked an enormous **(2)** .... forward in the development of wave power, which had tended to **(3)** .... behind its cousins in the other main **(4)** .... of renewable energy technology: wind power and solar power.

But surfers in the southwest **(5)** .... concerns about the project. Cornwall is Britain's principal surfing region **(6)** .... of the size of the Atlantic rollers hitting the beaches there, and surfers were concerned that the energy taken from the waves would **(7)** .... in a reduction of as much as 11 per cent in the height of those waves when they **(8)** .... the shore. But an independent study, which sought to reassure surfers that any effect on wave height would be more limited, has so far proved the project to be correct.

1	**A** came	**B** begun	**C** arrived	**D** started
2	**A** tread	**B** strike	**C** pace	**D** step
3	**A** lag	**B** leave	**C** drag	**D** delay
4	**A** limbs	**B** branches	**C** wings	**D** prongs
5	**A** explained	**B** spoke	**C** expressed	**D** commented
6	**A** because	**B** account	**C** reason	**D** thanks
7	**A** upshot	**B** result	**C** conclude	**D** arise
8	**A** succeeded	**B** realised	**C** reached	**D** achieved

TIP STRIP

Question 1: Only one of these words can be followed by the preposition *into*.

Question 5: Which of the words collocates with *concerns*?

Question 8: Which of the words means 'arrived at'?

Part 2

For questions **9 – 16**, read the text below and think of the word which best fits each gap. Use only **one** word in each gap. There is an example at the beginning (**0**).

In the exam, you write your answers **IN CAPITAL LETTERS on a separate answer sheet**.

Example: 0 T O

Spacemen's autographs

Only 12 astronauts actually set foot on the moon during the US Apollo space program between 1969 and 1972. According **(0)** .... Paul Prendergast, a postal worker from London, they are all pioneers who deserve more recognition for their outstanding achievement. Paul's fascination **(9)** .... the subject began in 2000 **(10)** .... he attended a convention for people **(11)** .... hobby is collecting autographs. There he met Alan Bean (the fourth person on the moon) and Ed Mitchell (the sixth). As he remembers: "There were television stars there, people from Bond movies and so **(12)** .... , but these men had walked on the moon. I headed straight **(13)** .... to meet them and ask for their autographs." For a collector, the challenge of trying to **(14)** .... hold of the remaining ten proved irresistible.

Yet Paul's quest was never going to be entirely straightforward. At that time, only nine of the astronauts were still alive and two **(15)** .... given up signing autographs years before. By establishing contacts with other collectors, however, and by buying from reputable dealers at specialist auctions, Paul did eventually **(16)** .... to achieve his goal.

TIP STRIP

Question 11: Which relative pronoun is needed here?

Question 12: Which preposition completes the fixed phrase that means the same as 'etc'?

Question 14: Which verb completes the multi-word verb meaning 'to obtain'?

Part 3

For questions **17 – 24**, read the text below. Use the word given in capitals at the end of some of the lines to form a word that fits in the gap **in the same line**. There is an example at the beginning (**0**).

In the exam, you write your answers **IN CAPITAL LETTERS on a separate answer sheet**.

Example: | 0 | E | X | C | A | V | A | T | I | O | N | | | | | |

The world's oldest perfume

The archaeologists working at an **(0)** .... on the island of Cyprus **EXCAVATE**
discovered the remnants of 14 different perfumes in a number of
bottles and other **(17)** .... at the site of an ancient perfumery. The **CONTAIN**
building was destroyed by an earthquake nearly 4,000 years ago, at
a time when Cyprus was already enjoying a **(18)** .... as a centre **REPUTED**
of perfume-making.

After undergoing scientific **(19)** .... , the perfumes were found to **ANALYSE**
contain a range of ingredients which would have been **(20)** .... **READY**
available in the immediate locality, including anise, pine, coriander,
lemon, bergamot and almond.

Having **(21)** .... what each perfume contained, the scientists then **IDENTITY**
set about remaking them using traditional techniques to find out what
they would actually have smelt like. They first **(22)** .... up the **GRIND**
extracts, then mixed them with olive oil in clay jugs before distilling
them. This method is the one recorded by writers in Ancient Roman
times. Although rather **(23)** .... by today's standards, the resulting **SOPHISTICATED**
aromas provide us with an olfactory window onto the ancient world,
and are evidence of the **(24)** .... skill employed by their creators. **CONSIDER**

TIP STRIP

Question 17: You need to add a suffix to this word to create a plural noun.

Question 20: You need to add two letters to make this adjective into an adverb.

Question 23: Add a negative prefix to this word.

Part 4

For questions **25 – 30**, complete the second sentence so that it has a similar meaning to the first sentence, using the word given. **Do not change the word given.** You must use between **three** and **six** words, including the word given. Here is an example (**0**).

Example:

0 Amy stayed at the hotel once before.

   FIRST

   This is .... Amy has stayed at the hotel.

The gap can be filled with the words 'not the first time that', so you write:

Example: | 0 | NOT THE FIRST TIME THAT |

In the exam, you write **only** the missing words **IN CAPITAL LETTERS on a separate answer sheet.**

---

25 There were a lot of things to think about before we made our decision.

   TAKEN

   Lots of things needed .... consideration before we could make our decision.

26 Could I ask you if you'd mind looking after my dog while I'm away?

   WONDERING

   I .... willing to look after my dog while I'm away?

27 I know that it was wrong of me to get angry in front of the children.

   LOST

   I know that I should .... in front of the children.

28 If you need any further information, please call me.

   HESITATE

   If you need any further information .... me a call.

29 It hasn't snowed quite as much this year as it did last year.

   SLIGHTLY

   This year, there has .... than there was last year.

30 Unless the team's performance improves, they may find they have to resign from the league.

   FORCED

   If the team's performance doesn't get .... resign from the league.

TIP STRIP

Question 25: Is the verb active or passive? Which preposition is used in this fixed phrase?

Question 27: You need an expression that means the same as 'got angry'.

Question 28: Which form of the verb follows 'hesitate'?

Part 5

You are going to read an article about an actress. For questions **31 – 36**, choose the answer (**A, B, C** or **D**) which you think fits best according to the text.

In the exam, you mark your answers **on a separate answer sheet.**

The voice of Bart Simpson

Clive Eyre remembers the day he met the actress who created the voice

The woman I'd come to meet was sitting atop a large plastic cow in the grounds of her Los Angeles home. Small and blonde, she held an umbrella and gave a mischievous smile for a photographer. "Hi, there!" she said, giving me a warm, almost motherly wave from her unusual vantage point. Her real name was Nancy Cartwright. Her stage name, however, was a little more familiar: Bart Simpson, the obnoxious, skateboard-touting ten-year-old from the cartoon metropolis of Springfield. It was hard to believe, but this middle-aged mother of two, dressed in a sensible green top and blue trousers, was the yellow-hued rascal who instructed the world to eat his shorts.

"I can bring him out at will," said Cartwright, with a hint of a raised eyebrow, her naturally husky voice always seemingly on the verge of breaking into a Bartism, punctuated by his cruel, gloating laughter. "Think about it, it's kind of ideal, isn't it? If I go to a party and someone brings a kid up to me I can go, 'Hey, man, what's happening?' and watch the kid's face. I love doing that." My own response was probably similar. The ten-year-old voice coming out of Cartwright was scarily incongruous. It belonged to another world – certainly not here in suburban LA, amongst the tennis courts and swimming pools. Reckless skateboarding certainly wouldn't be tolerated.

Cartwright, however, had grown tired of deploying Bart's voice as a means to claim traditional celebrity perks, such as a table at top restaurants. "I tried it once," she said. "It's embarrassing. People are like, 'So what?'" Following similarly disappointing encounters with unamused traffic cops and harried flight attendants, she learnt to relish her anonymous celebrity status. "It's probably because I have the choice whereas most celebrities don't," she concluded. "They're kind of, you know, at the whim of the public. That must be unnerving."

But there is, of course, something profoundly odd about the fact that Nancy Cartwright was at once both an A-list celebrity and a faceless nobody. So odd, in fact, that it inspired her to produce a one-woman show based on what she called 'My life as a ten-year-old boy'. The show took the audience through Cartwright's real life as a ten-year-old – living in the Midwestern 'nowheresville' of Dayton, Ohio – when she won a school competition with a performance of Rudyard Kipling's *How the Camel Got His Hump*. After that came other competitions, other trophies, and a gradual realisation that her voice was perfect for cartoons. By her late teens, Cartwright was working for a radio station where she met a Hollywood studio representative who gave her the name and phone number of Daws Butler, the legendary voice of cartoon favourites Huckleberry Hound and Yogi Bear.

At just 19, and with only that one contact, Cartwright, like so many wannabe starlets, packed her bags and headed west, transferring her university scholarship from Ohio to the University of California. Cartwright, however, was no ordinary blonde starlet. "Most people who come to Hollywood are looking to get on camera," she recalled. "My story's quite different. My purpose was to hook up with this pioneer of the voiceover industry, so that's what I did." He put her in touch with the directors at the Hanna-Barbera studio and helped her get the voice of Gloria in *Richie Rich* – the adventures of the richest boy in the world.

Then came the call from the producers of a 30-second cartoon spot on *The Tracey Ullman Show*. They wanted her to play the role of Lisa Simpson, a nerdy and morally upstanding know-all with a bratty little brother, Bart. "I went in, saw Lisa, and didn't really see anything I could sink my teeth into," says Cartwright.

"But the audition piece for Bart was right there, and I'm like, 'Whoa, ten years old, underachiever and proud of it!'", and I'm going, 'Yeah, man – that's the one I wanna do!'" She knew the audition was a success when Matt Greening, creator of *The Simpsons*, started cracking up and shouting, 'That's it! That's Bart!' It's no surprise to learn that Bart's catchphrase – "Eat my shorts!" – was originally an ad lib by Cartwright. The Bart voice had long been a part of Cartwright's repertoire, but it didn't come alive until she saw the pictures of him and read the script. The material, meanwhile, which was pretty heady stuff in the 1980s, didn't shock her. "You know what, I couldn't believe I was actually getting paid for doing things I'd get into trouble for doing as a kid."

31 The writer reveals that on meeting Nancy, he was

- **A** unprepared for her age.
- **B** struck by her ordinariness.
- **C** reassured by her appearance.
- **D** embarrassed by her behaviour.

32 How did adults tend to react when Nancy used Bart's voice in public?

- **A** They were confused by it.
- **B** They were unimpressed by it.
- **C** They gave her special treatment.
- **D** They accepted that she was a celebrity.

33 How did Nancy feel about keeping a relatively low profile?

- **A** nervous about the effects on her future career
- **B** unsure that it was a good choice to make
- **C** relieved not to be more in the public eye
- **D** sorry not to be recognised more often

34 What do we learn about Nancy's one-woman show?

- **A** It featured the wide range of voices she could produce.
- **B** It explored the strangeness of voiceover work.
- **C** It celebrated other famous cartoon characters.
- **D** It traced the development of her early career.

35 Why did Nancy originally decide to go to Hollywood?

- **A** She'd got a place on a course there.
- **B** She already had the offer of a job there.
- **C** Her ambition was to become a film star there.
- **D** There was somebody who could help her there.

36 Nancy got the part of Bart Simpson as a result of

- **A** volunteering to do an audition for it.
- **B** being rejected for the part of Bart's sister.
- **C** contributing to part of the script of the show.
- **D** successfully playing a male character in another show.

TIP STRIP

Question 32: Be careful. Nancy was hoping to get special treatment, but was she successful?

Question 35: Check the order of events carefully. Read to find her reasons for going rather than other details of her move or what other people do.

Question 36: Nancy originally auditioned for another part, but why didn't she play that part in the end?

Part 6

You are going to read four reviews of a collection of essays entitled *Why English?* For questions **37 – 40**, choose from the reviews **A – D**. The reviews may be chosen more than once.

In the exam, you mark your answers **on a separate answer sheet**.

Why English?

A

As the language of business and science, English is world's lingua franca. Hardly surprising, therefore, that ambitious parents see it as central to the curriculum of every sensible school. But the writers of the collection of essays *Why English?* see things differently. They make a convincing argument for the idea that the benefits of English to ordinary people — better jobs and access to new technologies – have been vastly overstated. Although there's some irony in the fact this collection is itself written in English, it does have much to recommend it. With educational institutions around the world all rushing to embrace English, it's appropriate to ask whether they're doing it well and for the right reasons. Mostly teachers themselves, the authors object, for example, to the practice of teaching children everything in English early on. They cite an impressive body of research that shows how subjects like maths and science are more effectively taught in the mother tongue.

B

The authors of *Why English?* stress that they aren't opposed to students learning English. This is just as well considering how much faith students' families place on its inclusion in school syllabuses. What they do correctly question, however, is the notion that knowledge of English is a social and economic necessity for all students, many of whom will rarely use it outside the classroom. What's more, they suggest that teaching other subjects in English to children from a young age can be counter-productive, although these claims aren't well supported. A number of the authors have classroom experience of teaching in English, and there's a tendency to fall back on anecdote rather than clear data about what is and isn't working. Furthermore, the very fact that the essays themselves are all written in English, clearly not the first language of most contributors, rather detracts from some of their main arguments.

C

A strong point of this collection of essays is that the writers all have first-hand experience of working in a language that isn't their mother tongue. The fact that the essays themselves are all written in English is testimony to the value of a lingua franca in facilitating the exchange of ideas. Less convincing is their contention that learning English may not open as many doors as governments and educationalists seem to believe. I think many people do regret the fact that their children are taught in English because it threatens the integrity and the standing of their own mother tongue, but they accept that they have little choice in the matter. Most of the essayists have worked as teachers themselves, and they bring this insight to their analysis of the various studies that have been conducted into the effects of teaching a range of subjects in English.

D

As anyone with teenage kids will tell you, whatever language they use at home, they want the kids to learn English at school. After all, these kids may need to study in English one day, or work in an English-speaking environment. The authors of this collection of essays seem to be suggesting that we've got this wrong somehow – that English isn't the passport to economic and social success anymore. But I don't see any evidence of that personally, and I had to smile when I saw that the collection itself is all written in that one language. Apart from this, however, the essays make for an interesting read. The authors are right to question some of our assumptions about the use of English across the curriculum and I was pleased to see so many relevant studies being quoted on both sides of the various arguments.

Which reviewer

has a different view from A regarding the attitude of parents to the role of English in the school curriculum?   37

expresses a similar view to B about the language in which the essays are written?   38

has a similar view to B regarding what the essayists say about the economic and social advantages of learning English?   39

expresses a different view to the others regarding how well the essayists' claims are backed up by research findings?   40

TIP STRIP

Question 37: Reviewer A thinks that most parents are happy for their children to be taught in English at school. Read to find out what the other reviewers think about this. Which one disagrees with A?

Question 38: Look at the end of B for this opinion.

Question 40: Look for words in the texts that relate to 'research findings'.

Part 7

You are going to read an extract from a newspaper article. Six paragraphs have been removed from the article. Choose from the paragraphs **A – G** the one which fits each gap (**41 – 46**). There is one extra paragraph which you do not need to use.

In the exam, you mark your answers **on a separate answer sheet**.

On a wing and a woof

Michael Cassell's close encounter with a paragliding puppy inspires a desire to try out the sport

I love dogs, but a dog's place is at your feet, not flying above your head. I was holidaying on the Côte d'Azure in France, and I couldn't quite believe what I was seeing. I think it was some form of terrier, although it was hard to tell because it wore goggles and a little bandana and was moving at some speed as it passed over the house.

41

I kept my eye on the pair and saw them land on the beach, where they received warm applause from early bathers. I'm sure they were breaking every rule in the book and if the police had intervened I imagine the dog at least could have lost his licence.

42

Paragliding, by contrast, relies entirely on thermic air and the skill of its pilot; to take to the skies on such a lightweight contraption is to soar free and silently in the arms of mother nature. The sport has spawned more than 650 clubs across France, and fans travel from across Europe to enjoy the mix of wild scenery and placid weather that the country offers. The most popular regions are the Alps, the Pyrenees and Corsica, and there are plenty of paragliding schools in those regions that will get beginners off the ground in two or three days.

43

The Côte d'Azure, however, is not in itself natural paragliding country, and we have found ourselves under the flight path of a growing number of enthusiasts simply because of the jagged ridge of red rock that towers 300 metres above sea level behind our house – the best jumping-off spot for miles around.

44

It's a 45-minute climb from the beach to this ridge-top and although the gliders weigh around seven kilos, there are a harness and helmet and boots and other bits and pieces to carry as well. I calculate that each flight lasts about four minutes and some of the keenest fans trudge past my gate three or four times a day. I tucked in behind one group to watch them get ready for the jump.

45

The reality, of course, is that with proper training and preparation paragliding is a very safe sport; there are accidents, but most are rarely that serious and usually occur on launching or landing. This group, however, knew their stuff. To forsake a long run and lift off for a virtual leap into space takes experience and supreme confidence.

46

I'm not a natural-born daredevil and wouldn't myself have found that experience thrilling. But I am nevertheless sorely tempted to have a go – maybe on a gently sloping hillside. "You'll need a medical certificate at your age," declared one of the group, instantly extinguishing the flame of adventure. But then if puppies can paraglide, why shouldn't an old dog like me?

TIP STRIP

Question 41: The first line of the article talks about 'the pair'. What is being referred to? Which option tells you more about the flying dog?

Question 43: The previous paragraph is talking about paragliding schools. Which of the options also talks about learning to paraglide?

Question 46: Look at the text after the gap. What does *that experience* refer to? Which of the options contains information about somebody having a thrilling experience?

A But this is no place for beginners. There are no gentle, grass-covered slopes to run down – the rocks are vertical and unyielding and anyone who leaps off them could easily get into difficulties unless they know what they're doing.

B For the more courageous, the pleasures of advanced thermalling await, but if you are of a more timid disposition and want to hold someone's hand, you can take a tandem course. If you are a dog, the experience must be like sticking your head out of the car window and letting the wind beat your ears round the back of your head.

C Not all of these untrained novices reach the beach, however. In recent days, one paraglider has landed on a neighbour's pool terrace, wrecking several terracotta pots and a previously unblemished flight record.

D Despite such unexpected intrusions on my privacy, I've decided that paragliding, with or without the canine companion, is immensely superior to microlight flying, in which the airborne are propelled by a motor so clamorous and noisy that any idea of soaring serenely through the heavens is soon lost.

E The biggest surprise was that they were not all strong, strapping young men, intent upon ticking off another item on some checklist of 'dangerous things to do before I die'. Of the six preparing to jump, three were women and the average age appeared to be somewhere in the mid-30s.

F The puppy was paragliding – a tiny, intrepid recruit to the sport that has taken off big time across the country. The creature was not on its own, thank goodness, but on a machine piloted by a young man who greeted me cheerily as they swooped beyond the end of the terrace and dived down the hillside.

G There was one nasty moment when one of the women leapt and, instead of instantly catching the air beneath her canopy, plunged alarmingly down the face of the cliff; but within seconds she had caught an updraft, and was whooping gleefully and on her way.

Part 8

You are going to read an article in which four readers suggest good places to go wildlife watching. For questions **47 – 56**, choose from the sections (**A – D**). The sections may be chosen more than once.

In the exam, you mark your answers **on a separate answer sheet.**

Which reader

feels that visiting the location has been a life-changing experience?	47
says the location may well become more renowned in the future?	48
got involved in activities designed to help various types of animal directly?	49
feels it unwise to bank on seeing one particular species?	50
mentions an abundance of animals belonging to one particular species?	51
mentions unpaid work being offered as part of a trip?	52
suffered some discomfort in order to witness one wildlife event?	53
mentions one particularly enjoyable form of transport?	54
points out the relative safety of an isolated location?	55
feels that independent travel is a realistic option in the area?	56

TIP STRIP

Question 48: Look for a phrasal verb that means 'become more popular'.

Question 54: Two of the readers mention a form of transport, but which clearly thinks it is enjoyable?

Question 55: You are looking for a reason why a wildlife encounter is not as potentially dangerous as you might think.

Wildlife encounters

Four readers suggest great locations where you can watch wildlife in its natural surroundings.

A   Kevin: Hallo Bay, Alaska

The first time you see a bear, when you realise that it's just you, the guide and that bear, your mouth definitely goes dry. Unlike those in other more frequently visited areas, the bears at Hallo Bay don't associate humans with food, as nobody's ever fed them, so they pose no risk. You can watch the bears fish in the river, nurse their cubs, photograph them hunting for clams on the beach or find them sleeping with their full bellies nestled in a hollow they've dug in the sand. For me, Hallo Bay's a magical place. I've always been a structured and organised person, but I've said for years now that I lost my list in Alaska. One special thing about Hallo Bay is that the remote camp has just a dozen guests at a time, with even smaller guided groups heading out in search of bears. And there's no shortage of them; Hallo Bay has one of the world's healthiest populations of coastal browns, maybe because of the plentiful food supply. It must be how the planet was several hundred years ago.

B   Sarah: Madikwe Game Reserve, South Africa

It's so hard to recommend just one location in Africa to go in search of the big five! However, if you've never been on safari before, then travel is straightforward in South Africa and its parks are the cheapest if you're short of money. The parks have well-equipped campsites and good-quality roads, so it's perfectly possible to fly in, hire a fully-equipped four-by-four, and head off on your own. There's also an impressive selection of volunteer projects involving animals, particularly around the country's biggest parks. I spent four weeks helping at a veterinary practice with African Conservation Experience. I got the chance to work with lions, cheetahs, sable antelopes, elephants and buffalo. The work's extremely hands-on and you have to be ready for anything, whether it's taking a lion's temperature or treating a dog for a snake bite!

C   Ray: Playa Grande Sanctuary, Costa Rica

Costa Rica's popularity as a wildlife venue could be about to take off, and deservedly so. It boasts the world's highest biodiversity with 850 species of birds and a quarter of the world's species of butterfly. From cloud forest to Caribbean beaches and from dry tropical forest to mangrove swamps, Costa Rica has it all: iguanas at your feet, capuchin monkeys overhead, sloths are to be seen, and if you're really lucky you'll catch sight of one of Costa Rica's jaguars. However, perhaps the most magical thing to do here is watch turtles lay their eggs on a moonlight-drenched beach. It does require patience; we waited two nights, napping on hard benches at the Playa Grande sanctuary, before one of the wardens shook us awake to say a female had been spotted laboriously making her way out of the surf. The turtles go into a sort of trance and we were allowed quite close to watch her dig a hole with her flippers and deposit hundreds of eggs, the size of golf balls, which are then gathered by the wardens and taken to their hatchery to protect them from predators.

D   Amy: Chitwan National Park, Nepal

With tigers, snow leopards, and one-horned rhinoceros, Nepal certainly has its share of endangered animals. The snow leopard is perhaps the most exotic of them all, but they're incredibly difficult to spot. Snow leopard treks are organized regularly but if you go on one, you need to enjoy it for the sheer magnificence of the scenery and not feel let down if you don't spot your ultimate prey. It could be a life-changing experience, but it's not that likely to happen. I visited Chitwan at the foot of the Himalayas, a park set aside for wildlife in 1959. It's the place to see Indian rhinoceros and is one of the last refuges of the Bengal tiger. One of the best ways to view both is from the back of an elephant – something that is rather fabulous in itself. We even got to help when two elephants were taken for their daily wash on the river bank near our hotel. It was one of the most amazing animal encounters possible, sitting on the backs of those huge elephants scrubbing their backs whilst they knelt in the water and sprayed us from their trunks!

GUIDANCE: WRITING

About the paper

There are two parts to the paper. In each part you have to complete one task. You have 1 hour 30 minutes to complete the whole paper.

Part 1
Part 1 is compulsory. You have to deal with prompts and opinions given in the task and write around 220–260 words in the form of an essay. You have to choose and discuss two from three points that you are given on a topic.

The focus of assessment is how well you present your arguments and achieve the task. You must cover both points you choose with enough detail to support your opinions.

It's not necessary to be too imaginative and invent a lot of extra detail, although you must support your arguments. Don't include things that are irrelevant.

Part 2
Part 2 has three questions, but you must choose only one to answer. You should write 220–260 words.

The questions may ask you to write a letter, an email, a proposal, a report or a review. In this part you can use your imagination to add detail to your answer.

How to do the paper

General points
- Spend at least 10 minutes planning your writing. Your answer should be well-organised with clear linking of ideas between sentences and paragraphs. In the exam you won't have enough time to write a rough answer and a final neat copy, but if you plan properly this won't be necessary.
- Make sure your writing is legible. If necessary, leave a line between paragraphs so that it is clear where one paragraph ends and the next begins.
- Everything you write should have a beginning, middle and an end. Remember to use an appropriate style and layout, both for the type of text, and the person you are writing to.
- Make sure you use a range of language, which includes vocabulary and structures. At this level, your language should not be too simple.
- Check that your answer is neither too long nor too short. If you write too much, you may include irrelevant information, which could have a negative effect on the target reader. If your answer is too short, you may not cover all the required points.
- Leave enough time to check your answer. Check grammar and spelling (you can use British or American spelling, but try not to mix them up). Make sure you've included all the points required to answer the question, and that you've included enough detail on each point. Check that you've included appropriate language functions required for the task, and you've also used a range of appropriate vocabulary and grammar.

Part 1
- Read the instructions carefully to clarify exactly what you have to do. Think about the three points you are given in the notes, and how much you could write for each one. Then choose which two to write about.
- You can use information from the opinions given if you like, but try not to use the same words.
- Decide on your conclusion and make notes on each point before you start to write. This will help you to write coherently.

Part 2
- Read through all the questions in Part 2. Before you choose which one to answer, think about what each task involves, so that you're confident you understand everything you have to do. Always check the context, reason for writing and the target reader. Each task has a given target reader and purpose which will determine what register and kind of language is appropriate for your answer.
- Think about what kind of writing you're best at. If you're good with more formal language and expressing your ideas concisely, you might consider writing a report or a proposal. If you're good at writing in an interesting way, you might choose a review. However, also consider whether you have enough ideas for the topic of each task. Don't just choose a task because you like the text type.

Part 1

You **must** answer this question. Write your answer in **220 – 260** words in an appropriate style.

In the exam, you write your answer **on a separate answer sheet**.

---

1   In class you have been discussing why many students have part-time jobs while they are at college. You have made the notes below:

> **Why college students have part-time jobs**
> - money
> - time
> - experience

> Some opinions expressed in the discussion:
>
> "Money's great but it isn't everything."
>
> "I'm so tired when I work and study together – nothing gets done well."
>
> "It'll stand me in good stead when I'm looking for a real job."

Write an essay discussing **two** of the reasons in your notes. You should **explain which reason is more influential** for college students who choose to have part-time jobs, **giving reasons** to support your answer.

You may, if you wish, make use of the opinions expressed in the debate, but you should use your own words as far as possible.

TIP STRIP

- In Part 1, you're given three points to think about. You choose two to discuss in your essay, and there are three quotes to give you more ideas. Don't write about more than two points.
- You must be clear in your mind exactly what the question is asking you to discuss. You're writing an essay, so you need to use a semi-formal style and organise your ideas into clear paragraphs.
- Spend time thinking about the notes and ideas you want to include. Then decide on your format – will you have one point per paragraph and discuss it, or will you write about both points in one paragraph and evaluate them both in the next?
- In this task you should choose two reasons and consider why students have part-time jobs. You should decide which reason you think is most influential before you start writing so that your argument will lead logically to your conclusion. For example, you could evaluate the pros and cons of time and money, and then decide which one has the most influence on students.
- Introduce the topic of the essay, and then consider each of your two chosen points. For example, you could discuss money by saying that it's difficult to manage without it, but on the other hand part-time jobs don't pay very much.
- If you choose the reason of 'time', talk about the need for students to have time to work but say that they can probably get the basics done and students do have a lot of holidays.
- If you choose the reason of 'experience', say that students need experience of the world of work, but part-time jobs may not carry much responsibility.
- State your conclusion clearly, which should come out of your evaluation of your two chosen points.
- Remember to use a range of language, and give examples or evidence to support your ideas.

Part 2

Write an answer to **one** of the questions **2 – 4** in this part. Write your answer in **220 – 260** words in an appropriate style. In the exam write your answer **on a separate answer sheet**, and put the question number in the box at the top of the page.

2   Your college wants to run a special event to provide advice and information about career and further education opportunities for students. The principal has asked students for proposals for the event outlining what should be included, suggesting how it should be organised and giving reasons for their recommendations.

Write your **proposal**.

3   An international book magazine has asked readers to send in reviews of books they think would be good to read on a long journey. Write a review of a book you feel would be especially good for a long journey, saying what you enjoyed about it and why you would recommend it to other travellers.

Write your **review**.

4   You have seen this announcement in a travel magazine:

Looking for adventure?

We need four people to take part in a television documentary called *Survival*. You'll live in a remote mountain area for three months with only your teammates for support. You'll keep a video diary of your experiences.

If you think you have the skills to live in a hostile environment and be a useful member of a team, write us a letter explaining why you should be included in the project.

Write your **letter**.

TIP STRIP

Question 2: A proposal is similar to a report in style and layout, but should focus on future recommendations.
- Use headings, bullet points, and a formal style.
- Summarise the proposal's purpose, give clear ideas, reasons and a conclusion.

Question 3: Reviews can be semi-formal or informal and include personal opinions. They usually entertain and inform the reader.
- Include both negative and positive points. Give a brief outline of the book, explain why you liked it and give reasons.

Question 4:
- Include reasons why you're suitable, in your letter using interesting language.
- Use paragraphs for each part with an appropriate greeting and ending.

GUIDANCE: LISTENING

About the paper

The Listening paper lasts for about 40 minutes. There are four parts and a total of 30 questions. You listen to texts of different types and different lengths, for example extracts from media broadcasts and podcasts as well as everyday conversations. You hear each recording twice and you have time to read the questions before you listen.

Part 1
Listen to three unrelated extracts of around one minute each. Each extract has two speakers. You have to answer two three-option multiple-choice questions on each extract. The three extracts aren't linked, and there are a variety of contexts and interaction patterns.

Part 2
You listen to one long monologue of around two to three minutes in which the speaker is talking about a particular subject. A set of eight sentences reports the speaker's main points. A word or short phrase has been removed from each sentence. You have to listen and complete the gaps.

Part 3
In Part 3, you will hear a one long interview or discussion of around four minutes. You have to answer six four-option multiple-choice questions.

Part 4
You hear a series of five short monologues on a theme. Each monologue lasts around 30 seconds. You have to complete two tasks as you listen. Each task has eight options (A–H). As you listen, you match one option from Task 1 and one option from Task 2 to each speaker. You should try to match the ideas that the speakers express to the wording of the options.

How to do the paper

Part 1
- Before you listen to each extract, you hear the context sentence. Think about who the speakers are and what you're going to hear. For example, is it an interview, an informal conversation, etc.?
- You have time to read the two questions. Underline the main words and ideas in each question stem and options (A–C).
- The question often tells you which of the speakers, the man the woman or both, you need to listen to when you answer each of the questions.
- The first time you listen, find the correct answer to the question posed in the question stem.
- The second time you listen, choose the option which matches your answer.
- The wording of the options doesn't repeat the vocabulary and expressions used by the speakers. You need to match the meaning of ideas expressed in the recording to the wording of the questions.

Part 2
- Before you listen, you hear the context sentence. Think about the person who's speaking and the topic you're going to hear about.
- You have 45 seconds to read through the sentences before you listen. Think about the type of information that's missing in each of the sentences.
- Most answers are concrete pieces of information, e.g. proper nouns (names, places, etc.).
- The sentences you read are in the same order as the information you hear. Use the sentences to help you keep your place as you are listening.
- You hear the words you need to write on the recording. There's no need to change the form of the word or to find a paraphrase.
- You should write no more than three words in each gap. Most answers are single words or compound nouns.
- Check that your answer fits the sentence grammatically and makes sense in the complete sentence.

Part 3
- Before you listen, you hear the context sentence. Think about the people who are speaking and the topic you're going to hear about.
- You have 70 seconds to read through the questions before you listen to the conversation.
- Underline the main words and ideas in each question stem and the options (A–D).
- The questions follow the order of information you hear when you listen. Listen out for key vocabulary and ideas that introduce the topic of each question that you have to answer. These are often in the interviewer's questions.
- The question often tells you which of the speakers, the man the woman or both, you need to listen to when you answer each of the questions.
- The first time you listen, find the correct answer to the question posed in the question stem.
- The second time you listen, choose the option which matches your answer.
- The wording of the options doesn't repeat the vocabulary and expressions used by the speakers. You need to match the meaning of ideas expressed in the recording to the wording of the questions.

Part 4
- There are five monologues on a theme. In each monologue, you hear a different speaker. You hear all five speakers once, then the series is repeated.
- Before you listen, you hear the context sentence and the instructions for each of the two tasks. Think about the topic you're going to hear about, and the ideas you have to listen for.
- You have 45 seconds to read through the two tasks before you listen. Read the options (A–H) in both tasks so that you're ready to choose one from each set for each speaker as you listen.
- The first time you listen, pay attention to the speaker's main idea. Mark the option closest to this idea.
- The second time you listen, check your answers. You may need to change some of them. Remember that in each task there are three options that you don't need to use.
- Don't worry if you don't understand every word. If you're not sure of an answer, then guess. You've probably understood more than you think.

Part 1

You will hear three different extracts. For questions **1 – 6**, choose the answer (**A**, **B** or **C**) which fits best according to what you hear. There are two questions for each extract.

In the exam, you write your answers **on a separate answer sheet**.

Extract One

You hear two guests on a chat show discussing travel and holidays.

1   What do they agree about?

   A   Watching television can spoil a holiday.
   B   Holidays are for getting away from it all.
   C   It's important not to lose touch with reality on holiday.

2   How does the woman feel about travelling?

   A   It's always enjoyable.
   B   It is not the best part of a holiday.
   C   It generally makes her feel restless.

Extract Two

You hear part of an interview with a Formula One racing driver.

3   What does the driver say about keeping fit?

   A   Working out in the gym tends to bore him.
   B   Playing other sports helps develop key muscles.
   C   Driving is actually a good way to maintain general fitness.

4   In his opinion, what makes a great Formula One driver?

   A   an outstanding natural ability behind the wheel
   B   enough mechanical knowledge to help design cars
   C   the flexibility to perform well in a range of vehicles

---

TIP STRIP

Question 1: Listen for when the woman uses the word *also*. This is when she agrees with him.

Question 4: Listen for the phrase that means 'most important'.

Question 6: Listen for the word *finalists*. The answer comes after this.

Extract Three

You hear a radio announcement about a writing competition.

5   The presenter says that each of the finalists in the competition will

    A   win a money prize.
    B   be invited to a prestigious event.
    C   have their story published in the press.

6   Moira advises those entering the competition to

    A   write about their own life and experiences.
    B   base their story on one by a well-known writer.
    C   avoid being over-ambitious in the scope of the story.

Part 2

You will hear an outdoor activities trainer called Eric Duncan giving a presentation about trekking in the Himalayas. For questions **7 – 14**, complete the sentences with a word or short phrase.

In the exam, you mark your answers **on a separate answer sheet**.

TREKKING IN THE HIMALAYAS

Eric says that you need neither experience nor an especially

(7) .... nature to go on these treks.

Eric recommends the months of (8) .... and ....

for trekking in the region.

Eric reminds us that we shouldn't regard the trek as a (9) ....

Trekking in Nepal can sometimes feel like walking through

(10) .... , as a result of altitude.

Eric says that many people buy a (11) ....

that is not good enough.

Eric says that organising an independent trek can be

(12) .... as well as saving money.

Eric points out that a guide will often also work as a

(13) .... if needed.

Eric recommends finding a guide through a local (14) ....

TIP STRIP

Question 11: Various pieces of equipment are mentioned, but which does he say are the commonest problem?

Question 12: You are listening for an adjective here.

Question 13: What other role might a guide perform? Listen to check your predictions.

Part 3

You will hear an interview with a comedian called Kevin Burke. For questions **15 – 20**, choose the answer (**A**, **B**, **C** or **D**) which fits best according to what you hear.

In the exam, write your answers **on a separate answer sheet**.

---

15 When it is suggested that he isn't really as happy as he appears, Kevin

    A admits that he conforms to a stereotype.
    B explains why people might assume that.
    C accepts that he's an untypical comedian.
    D confirms that depression can be a problem.

16 What does Kevin value most about the book entitled *Laughter*?

    A It was written with comedians in mind.
    B It helps him see why some comedians fail.
    C It shows him why audiences react as they do.
    D It aims to show what makes certain jokes funny.

17 What does Kevin say about his time at university?

    A He regrets his choice of degree subject.
    B He's proud of his academic achievements.
    C He enjoyed getting involved in a range of activities.
    D He had a lot in common with other students on his course.

18 After leaving university, Kevin

    A was determined to build a career as a journalist.
    B didn't really enjoy the type of work he was doing.
    C set his sights on getting work as a television presenter.
    D took the opportunity to develop his skills as a performer.

19 What does Kevin say about his television career?

    A It's not where he does his best work.
    B He wishes he hadn't accepted certain offers.
    C It's not as demanding as working on stage with a live audience.
    D He feels most comfortable doing a range of different programmes.

20 Kevin believes that he is successful on stage because

    A he's able to make audiences feel sorry for him.
    B he can convince audiences that he's in control.
    C he's able to laugh at his own appearance.
    D he can appeal to people's sense of logic.

TIP STRIP

Question 15: Listen to Kevin's whole answer. Is he a happy person or not?

Question 17: Listen for the interviewer's question about university – Kevin's answer follows.

Question 18: Listen for Kevin's attitudes towards the different types of work he did in this period.

Part 4

You will hear five short extracts in which people are talking about training courses they have done recently.

In the exam, mark your answers **on a separate answer sheet.**

TASK ONE

For questions **21 – 25**, choose from the list (**A – H**) the reason each speaker gives for choosing their particular course.

TASK TWO

For questions **26 – 30**, choose from the list (**A – H**) the main thing each person says they have gained from their course.

While you listen you must complete both tasks.

A	a colleague's recommendation	
B	an advertisement	Speaker 1 — 21
C	a trainer's advice	Speaker 2 — 22
D	a chance meeting	Speaker 3 — 23
E	a management suggestion	Speaker 4 — 24
F	a review on a website	Speaker 5 — 25
G	a newspaper article	
H	a friend's experience	

A	greater confidence at work	
B	better promotion prospects	Speaker 1 — 26
C	greater respect in the office	Speaker 2 — 27
D	a more varied workload	Speaker 3 — 28
E	more opportunities for travel	Speaker 4 — 29
F	an improved salary package	Speaker 5 — 30
G	the chance to work on new projects	
H	contacts with useful people	

TIP STRIP

Speaker 1: Be careful, the speaker mentions an advertisement, but it's not the answer to 21.
Speaker 2: Listen for how the speaker felt afterwards – it will give the answer to 27.
Speaker 3: Listen for who recommended the course – this helps with the answer to 23.
Speaker 4: Listen for the phrase *I was right* – the answer to 29 comes just after it.

GUIDANCE: SPEAKING

About the paper

The Speaking test takes 15 minutes and there are four parts. You take the test with a partner. There are two examiners, although only one (the Interlocutor) speaks to you. The other examiner listens and gives detailed marks.

Part 1
Part 1 takes about two minutes. First the interlocutor asks each of you direct questions asking for personal information. Then the interlocutor asks you and your partner questions in turn on general topics such as your interests, daily routines and likes and dislikes.

Part 2
Part 2 takes about four minutes, and you each speak on your own for about a minute. You're given three photographs. You compare two of the pictures and say something more about them. You're also asked a question about your partner's photographs after he or she has finished.

Part 3
Part 3 is divided into two parts, and lasts around four minutes. You discuss a task with your partner for around two minutes, using ideas you're given as prompts or ideas on a mind map. After two minutes the interlocutor asks you a second question, which isn't written down, and you have to reach a decision together related to the topic you've been discussing. You have a minute for this.

Part 4
Part 4 takes around five minutes. The Interlocutor leads a general discussion that broadens the topic of the Part 3 task by asking you more abstract questions on related issues.

How to do the paper

Part 1
- For the initial questions asking for personal information, you only need to give short answers; don't prepare long speeches about who you are and where you're from, but try to say more than yes or no.
- In the rest of Part 1, you'll be asked about your ideas and opinions on general topics, such as what you enjoy or how you spend your free time. Think of this as being similar to meeting someone in a social situation. You should provide enough detail to give interesting answers, without monopolising the time.

Part 2
- Listen to the interlocutor's instructions carefully. The task is also written on the paper above the photographs so you won't forget what you have to do.
- You can ask the Interlocutor to repeat the task if you have to, but only do this if it is really necessary as you will lose time.
- Compare the pictures first and then move on to the second part of the task. Don't describe the pictures; describing them won't allow you to show a range of language at the right level.
- Listen to what your partner says about their pictures, because the interlocutor will ask you a short question about them. In your answer to this question you should give some detail, but be careful not to say too much as you only have a short time for this.

Part 3
- Listen to the task carefully so that you understand exactly what to do. The task is written in the middle of the paper with the written prompts around it, and you have a short time to read them before you have to start talking. You can ask the Interlocutor to repeat the task if you're not sure, or check what you have to do with your partner, but this should not be necessary.
- Discuss each written prompt in turn. It doesn't matter if you don't discuss all the prompts, so make sure you say everything you can think of about each one before you move on to the next. Try to discuss the issues raised in the prompt in detail, and try to use a range of language.
- Remember to ask your partner for their views as well as giving your own opinion. Really listen to what they say so that you can respond to their ideas and suggestions appropriately.
- After two minutes the interlocutor stops you and asks a second question which involves making a decision on a topic related to the one you've been discussing. This question isn't written on the paper.
- Continue to use a range of language in your discussion and don't reach a decision too quickly, or you won't talk for a minute. Remember, there's no 'right' decision.

Part 4
- The Interlocutor may ask questions for you both to discuss, or ask you each a question in turn. You can contribute to your partner's question, as long as you do this appropriately.
- The questions in this part are more abstract, and you should give longer answers than you did in Part 1. Try to develop your ideas, and give your opinions in an interesting and coherent way.
- You can disagree with what your partner says! There are no 'right' answers to the questions.

TEST 1 SPEAKING

Part 1 (2 minutes)

The examiner will ask you one or two questions about yourself and what you think about everyday topics such as work or study, travel, holidays, daily life and routines. For example:

- Do you prefer to study in the morning, or the evening? (Why?)
- What kind of job would you like to do in the future? (Why?)
- Do you like to follow a routine, or are you a spontaneous person? (Why?)
- What kind of holidays do you enjoy most? (Why?)
- What's your favourite way of travelling? (Why?)
- Do you read any newspapers or magazines regularly? (Why / Why not?)
- Do you use the internet much in your daily life? (Why / Why not?)
- What do you enjoy doing with friends at the weekend? (Why?)

Part 2 (4 minutes)

STRETCHING

Turn to the pictures on page 170. They show people stretching in different situations.

(Candidate A), I'd like you to compare **two** of the pictures, and say **why the people might want to stretch in these situations, and how important it might be for them to stretch properly**.

(Candidate B), who do you think might find stretching most difficult? (Why?)

PEOPLE WITH SCREENS

Turn to the pictures on page 172. They show people with screens in different situations.

(Candidate B), compare **two** of the pictures and say **why the screens might be important to the people and how difficult it would be for the people to manage without them**.

(Candidate A), which screen do you think is easiest to use? (Why?)

TIP STRIP

Part 1:
Give answers that tell the examiner about you and your personal opinions. There's no 'right' answer, so try to give details that are interesting. Don't monopolise the time. Think of this as meeting someone for the first time socially.

For the first four questions you could say:

- I'm very much a morning person – I do all my studying then because I find it easier to concentrate.
- I'd love to be a teacher – I think it would be a very rewarding job. I'm good with children.
- I'm pretty spontaneous – I think life is boring if you always know what's going to happen.
- I prefer visiting different places. I'm not keen on lazing around on the beach. It's a waste of time.

TIP STRIP

Part 2:
Stretching
Candidate A, you could say: *people need to stretch for different reasons, such as staying mobile in old age or keeping flexible on a long journey … it's important to stretch properly if you're doing an exercise, but not so much on a flight … it's important not to overstretch … it's better to do it with an expert when you're older.*
Candidate B, don't say too much, but give details, e.g. *I think it's hard to stretch on a plane because there's no room in the aisle.*

People with screens
Candidate B, you could say: *screens are great for keeping in touch with family … it's hard to see performers in a live concert without them … a screen makes business presentations more effective … they can be difficult to manipulate … people could use a phone instead.*
Candidate A, you could say: *It seems to me that the easiest screen to use is the family's because they're just talking, not presenting anything.*

Part 3 (4 minutes)

Now I'd like you to talk together for about two minutes

Here are some ways that students can find out about career options and a question for you to discuss. First you have some time to look at the task. *[Turn to the task on page 171]*

Now talk to each other about **the advantages and disadvantages for students of finding out about career options in these ways**.

Thank you.

Now you have a minute to decide **which way is the most effective for students to get the best information**.

Part 4 (5 minutes)

Answer these questions.

- Which is more important for young people leaving school nowadays: going to college or getting a job? (Why?)
- Some people say it's pointless to study academic subjects because vocational subjects are more useful. Do you agree? (Why / Why not?)
- Some people decide on their career at a very early age. Do you think this is a good idea? (Why / Why not?)
- Do you think technology has significantly changed the way people work? (Why /Why not?)
- Some people do the same job all their lives, and others change many times. Which do you think is better? (Why?)
- Which is more important when choosing a career, the salary or the work? (Why?)

Select any of the following prompts, as appropriate:
- What do you think?
- Do you agree?
- How about you?

TIP STRIP

Part 3:

Read the prompts and consider the pros and cons of each one in detail. Focus your discussion on assessing each one in depth before you move on to the next. Remember there's no right answer, and it's better to use complex language exploring one idea in detail than to rush round all of them.

You could say: *you might find things you hadn't thought about on the internet but you can't ask questions ... teachers know about academic qualifications but may be aware of much more ... parents have a vested interest in helping you but their advice could be biased.*

TIP STRIP

Part 4:

Consider the more abstract issues behind the questions, which in this task focus on work and careers. Give reasons for your opinions, and remember that you can include your partner in the discussion.

You could say:
- There are pros and cons to both of them – if you get a job you earn money immediately but there may not be future prospects, but if you go to college it's expensive and you're not guaranteed a job.
- Vocational subjects will get you a job, but it may not be very intellectually satisfying and you may be closing down your options for the rest of your life.
- It's always better to keep your options open – if you decide too young then you may not accept other suggestions and miss out on something that could be good. On the other hand, if you're dedicated to being something like a dancer then you must start training very young.
- People often work from home, which has dramatically changed the way they work – they don't have to go in to an office every day. People can work seven days a week if they want, which may not create a healthy work/life balance.
- I think they both have advantages and disadvantages. If you don't change then you can get stale, but you become a real expert in your job. If you keep changing you gain a lot of different experience, but may never become a real specialist.
- Of course many people will say the salary! But actually if you're bored at work, even if you're earning a lot of money, it's very frustrating and probably not healthy in the long-term.

PRACTICE TEST 2 WITH GUIDANCE

PARTS 1-4

READING AND USE OF ENGLISH

Testing focus

Part 1
In Part 1, there is a range of testing focuses. Most questions focus on your knowledge of vocabulary and how words are used. Questions may focus on:
- your knowledge of general vocabulary related to the topic.
- the relationship between words, e.g. which preposition is used after a word, or whether it's followed by an infinitive or a gerund.
- your knowledge of collocation, e.g. which words are often used together to express a particular idea.
- your knowledge of fixed expressions, including phrasal verbs.
- your knowledge of linking words and phrases. This tests whether you've understood the meaning of a whole paragraph or the meaning of the text as a whole.

Part 2
Part 2 mostly tests your knowledge of grammar and sentence structure. Questions can focus on:
- the relationship between words, e.g. which words go together to form a fixed expression or phrasal verb.
- sentence structure, e.g. asking you to insert the correct relative pronoun or a conjunction.
- other grammatical words, e.g. quantifiers, determiners, articles, etc.
- linking words and phrases to test whether you've understood the meaning of the whole text.

Part 3
Part 3 tests whether you can create the correct form of the word to fit in the sentence. Questions may focus on:
- your knowledge of prefixes and suffixes.
- your grammatical knowledge, e.g. which form of the word is needed to complete the meaning in the sentence.
- common expressions and collocations, e.g. which form of the word is used in a particular context.
- your knowledge of compound words.

Part 4
Part 4 tests both your grammatical and lexical knowledge. Questions always have two testing points, e.g. a change to a word from the input sentence, plus a change to the word order to create a new sentence pattern.
- You're tested on your ability to express the same ideas using different grammatical forms and patterns, e.g. in a sentence that starts with a different word, or using a different part of speech.
- Questions may test your knowledge of fixed phrases and collocations by asking you to find the words that combine with those already in the target sentence.
- Your answer must be grammatically accurate.

Preparation

- Do as many practice tests as possible so that you fully understand what's expected of you and you feel confident going into the exam.
- Keep a vocabulary notebook where you can write down any useful vocabulary you come across, arranged by topic.
- Try to learn words in chunks rather than in isolation. When you learn a new word, keep a record of both the word and the sentence it's used in.
- When you're doing practice tests, keep a note of items you get wrong and attempt to do them again two weeks later.
- Write a verb on one side of a card, and its dependent preposition on the other. Test yourself on them in your free time.
- Choose a text in English and underline all the prepositions. Then go back through and decide which ones are part of set word patterns.
- Go through a reading text and write a list of all the adjectives. Is there a noun in the same family? What about a verb?

Testing focus

Part 5
Part 5 tests your detailed understanding of the meaning of the text, as well as general language and reading skills. Most questions relate to specific pieces of text. There is a range of testing focuses in Part 5 questions. For example, some questions focus on a phrase or sentence in the text, whilst others ask you to interpret the meaning of a whole paragraph.

Look for clues in the question stems to help you find the targeted piece of text. For example, 'In the third paragraph' is a clear indication of the piece of text you need to read; but it also tells you not to consider information and ideas from elsewhere in the text when choosing your answer.

Some questions focus on the attitude and opinions of the writer. Other questions may focus on the views of other people mentioned in the text. Some questions focus on the language that the writer has used to express his or her ideas, e.g. choice of vocabulary and expression, use of pronouns and other stylistic features.

Part 6
Part 6 tests your ability to read what different writers say about the same topic or ideas, and understand whether they hold the same or different views about the specific issues raised.
- Some questions test your ability to see which two writers hold the same or different views, but other questions focus on which writer holds a different view to the other three.
- Look for the cues in the question stems that tell you what to look for, e.g. 'Which writer shares writer A's opinion about …'. This means that you need to find the opinion in section A, and read it carefully to understand the opinion being expressed. Then you should read the other three sections to find where similar ideas are discussed. Then you need to find the writer who expresses the same opinion as A.

Part 7
Part 7 tests your ability to see the links between the different parts of a text and use these to put a jumbled text into the correct order. This means looking for the links the writer makes between paragraphs in order to tell the story, or develop the argument coherently. These links can be of different types and, often, more than one type of link helps you to answer the question. Look for:
- vocabulary links between the paragraphs, especially where an idea from one paragraph is developed in the following one. Don't expect to see exactly the same words used, however. You should look for different words with a similar meaning.
- grammatical links between the paragraphs, especially the use of pronouns and other words that summarise or refer to things already mentioned.
- logical links of topic and focus. Look for where people, places or ideas are introduced in the base text. If these are referred to in an option, then that paragraph must fit later in the text.

You're looking for links that work, but also looking for links that don't work. For example, a paragraph in the options may seem to fit a gap logically, and may contain the right sort of ideas and vocabulary, but you still need to check all the pronouns to make sure they have a point of reference in the text before the gap. If they don't, then the paragraph doesn't fit and you need to keep looking through the other options.

Part 8
In Part 8, you're being tested on your ability to locate relevant parts of the text, or texts, and match them to the ideas in the question prompts. Two types of reading skill are involved:
- the ability to read through a text, understand how it's organised and locate the parts relevant to a particular prompt. This involves reading quickly to get a general idea of the text, without worrying about the meaning of every word or the exact point being made by the writer.
- the skill of careful reading to understand the precise meaning in both the question prompt and in the relevant part of the base text. The question prompt reports ideas from the text, but doesn't use exactly the same vocabulary and ideas to do this. You have to think about the exact meaning to find the correct match.

Preparation

- Do as many practice tests as possible so that you fully understand what's expected of you, and you feel confident going into the exam.
- Remember that the Cambridge Advanced exam aims to test real-life skills. The reading that you do outside the classroom will help you become a more fluent reader.
- To help with Parts 5 and 8, read texts which express people's attitudes and opinions, such as interviews with famous people, commentaries on current affairs, reports of scientific discoveries, etc. and concentrate on understanding what different people think about the issues raised.
- Read news stories and reviews on a range of websites to see what different writers think about the same topic. Look for whether they agree or disagree. This will help you in Part 6.
- Look at English-language news articles and note down the words and phrases used to link the paragraphs. This will help you with Part 7 in particular.
- Practise reading texts quickly all the way through to understand the gist. You could read online articles and summarise the main ideas or opinions in them.

Part 1

For questions **1 – 8**, read the text below and decide which answer (**A**, **B**, **C** or **D**) best fits each gap. There is an example at the beginning (**0**).

In the exam, you mark your answers **on a separate answer sheet**.

Example:
0   **A** recognises   **B** believes   **C** agrees   **D** approves

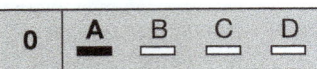

The texting pigeons

Not everybody **(0)** .... the benefits of new developments in communications technology. So widespread has texting become, however, that even pigeons have started doing it. Twenty of the birds are about to **(1)** .... to the skies with the task of measuring air pollution, each **(2)** .... with sensor equipment and a mobile phone. The **(3)** .... made by the sensors will be automatically **(4)** .... into text messages that will **(5)** .... on a dedicated 'pigeon blog'.

The birds will also each have a GPS receiver and a camera to capture aerial photos, and researchers are building a tiny 'pigeon kit' containing all these **(6)** .... , which each bird will carry in a miniature backpack, **(7)** .... , that is, from the camera, which will hang around its neck.

The data the pigeons text will be displayed in the **(8)** .... of an interactive map, which will provide local residents with up-to-the-minute information on their local air quality.

1	**A** make	**B** launch	**C** reach	**D** take
2	**A** armed	**B** loaded	**C** granted	**D** stocked
3	**A** studies	**B** readings	**C** reviews	**D** inquiries
4	**A** adapted	**B** converted	**C** revised	**D** applied
5	**A** attend	**B** present	**C** issue	**D** appear
6	**A** gadgets	**B** utensils	**C** appliances	**D** implements
7	**A** instead	**B** except	**C** apart	**D** besides
8	**A** shape	**B** way	**C** form	**D** size

TIP STRIP

Question 3: This is a collocation. Which word is used to talk about what 'sensors' do?

Question 6: All the words have a similar meaning, but only one is the correct word for the context.

Question 7: Read beyond the gap. Only one of these linking words is followed by the preposition *from*.

Part 2

For questions **9 – 16**, read the text below and think of the word which best fits each gap. Use only **one** word in each gap. There is an example at the beginning (**0**).

In the exam, you write your answers **IN CAPITAL LETTERS** on a separate answer sheet.

Example: 0 C A M E

A computer bag with style

It **(0)** .... as something as a surprise in the fashion industry when Julien MacDonald, the well-known dress designer, teamed **(9)** .... with the company Intel to produce a computer bag. MacDonald made his name creating the type of dresses that major celebrities like to be seen wearing at high-profile events such as film premieres and awards ceremonies.

The computer bag, however, was not designed with such occasions **(10)** .... mind. Rather it was created for the modern woman **(11)** .... relies on technology but hopes to look more chic than geek. MacDonald first got inspiration for the bag **(12)** .... he caught sight of female friends and colleagues at fashion shows, furiously typing away on their laptops. He couldn't **(13)** .... noticing, however, that the rather unstylish carrying cases needed to transport the machines tended to get pushed **(14)** .... of sight under their chairs. It was as **(15)** .... the women were somehow ashamed of them. MacDonald **(16)** .... out to change all that.

TIP STRIP

Question 9: You need a preposition to complete the phrasal verb.

Question 11: A relative pronoun is needed here.

Question 13: This is a fixed expression. What is the verb needed to complete it?

Part 3

For questions **17 – 24**, read the text below. Use the word given in capitals at the end of some of the lines to form a word that fits in the gap **in the same line**. There is an example at the beginning (**0**).

In the exam, you write your answers **IN CAPITAL LETTERS** on a separate answer sheet.

Example: | 0 | A | T | T | R | A | C | T | I | O | N | | | | | |

What makes a great waterfall?

One of the world's best-known waterfalls is Niagara Falls, on the US-Canadian border, which has been a major tourist **(0)** .... for over a century. The astonishing thing about Niagara's fame, however, is how **(17)** .... it is. Niagara is nowhere near the biggest waterfall in the world, nor is it the tallest waterfall in the US. — **ATTRACT** / **RATED**

So what is it that makes a waterfall the best? It isn't its **(18)** .... There are many **(19)** .... tall waterfalls, some cascading thousands of feet, such as Norway's Strupenfossen, but these aren't the most visited. It seems that when people go to see a waterfall, they expect to see a serious amount of water, and what is **(20)** .... is that Niagara is the biggest waterfall in North America in terms of volume, and this perhaps explains its **(21)** .... appeal. — **HIGH** / **CREDIBLE** / **DISPUTE** / **ENDURE**

Tourists who appreciate waterfalls for their sheer **(22)** .... beauty, however, know that Niagara's continental neighbour, Iguacu Falls, on the border of Brazil and Argentina, is by far the most **(23)** .... Iguacu's pristine **(24)** .... setting makes it one of the planet's great natural wonders. — **BREATH** / **SPECTACLE** / **TROPIC**

TIP STRIP

Question 17: You need to add a prefix to create a word which means 'given too much credit'.

Question 18: What is the noun of 'high'? Be careful to spell the word correctly.

Question 20: You need to add a prefix and a suffix to this word to create a negative adjective.

Part 4

For questions **25 – 30**, complete the second sentence so that it has a similar meaning to the first sentence, using the word given. **Do not change the word given**. You must use between **three** and **six** words, including the word given. Here is an example (**0**).

Example:

0 Amy stayed at the hotel once before.

   FIRST

   This is ………………………………………… Amy has stayed at the hotel.

The gap can be filled with the words 'not the first time that', so you write:

Example: | 0 | *NOT THE FIRST TIME THAT*

In the exam, you write **only** the missing words **IN CAPITAL LETTERS on a separate answer sheet**.

---

25 Playing the drums is fun, but so is singing in a choir.

   JUST

   It's …………………………… singing in a choir as it is playing the drums.

26 I don't much like the look of those sandwiches.

   APPEAL

   Those sandwiches …………………………… very much.

27 Phil is likely to get the job that he's being interviewed for.

   CHANCES

   The …………………………… the job he's being interviewed for.

28 Everybody says Tom's grandfather was an extremely skilful chess player.

   SUPPOSED

   Tom's grandfather is …………………………… an extremely skilful chess player.

29 The teacher tried to attract our attention, but we all ignored her.

   TOOK

   The teacher tried to attract our attention, but none of …………………………… her.

30 It's important to consider everyone's opinion before a final decision is made.

   ACCOUNT

   Everyone's opinion must …………………………… before a final decision is made.

TIP STRIP

Question 25: Look for a comparative structure.

Question 27: Which phrase with *chances* means the same as 'is likely to'?

Question 30: You need a passive construction.

Part 5

You are going to read an article about a fashion model. For questions **31 – 36**, choose the answer (**A**, **B**, **C** or **D**) which you think fits best according to the text.

In the exam, you mark your answers **on a separate answer sheet**.

Model citizen

An interview with the supermodel Helen Blakemore.

Helen Blakemore is curled up in a chair in an office at Models Live, the agency that represents her. You hear a lot about Helen being 'a freak of nature', and she can look so extraordinary on the catwalk – all jutting hips, jagged nose and towering height. But here she is in person – the muse to many a top fashion designer – a delicate, pretty woman, not that tall after all, but effortlessly stylish in jeans and a stripey top, her cropped hair pulled back, in an orange scarf. At first, when you arrive in the room, you could be forgiven for taking her for an assistant if a second look didn't reveal her prettiness: "Gosh aren't you beautiful," I say, sort of to apologise, and blow me if the woman who's launched a thousand shows doesn't blush.

In her eleven years on the catwalk and on magazine covers, Helen has accrued extraordinary personal wealth, but despite having been 'the face' of many top brands, she's managed to keep her profile relatively low. Even more admirably, in an industry renowned for its bitchiness ("you have to take it head on" she confides), she has kept a reputation as 'the nice face of fashion'. She was one of the girls followed in the TV documentary about modelling, and was breathtakingly level-headed and amusing in it.

As a friend to another model who has admitted to anorexia, Helen has talked cogently about the responsibility the industry has towards both models and the girls who try to emulate them. She's keen to foster a better relationship with the press ("at the moment they want to vilify or victimise us"), she gives talks to each year's new faces and, through the BFC, helps allocate sponsorship to new designers. And the reason she's agreed to a rare interview is that she's appearing in, and helping to plan, the opening of a music festival in London and a star-studded catwalk show that will benefit two leading charities.

Helen Blakemore grew up in provincial England, the middle of three girls. She was training to be a nursery nurse and "struggling through her final year at school" when she was spotted at a local fashion show. She's talked a lot about how uncomfortable she was with her body when she was growing up. "I outgrew my dad when I was 17. I outgrew everyone: aunties, sisters, mother, boyfriends." Success wasn't immediate, but years of ballet classes meant she was a natural on the catwalk. "Walking in heels felt like a holiday after pointes." Her big breakthrough didn't come until one day, on a shoot in Brazil, she chopped off her long hair. "I found my femininity for the first time, my version of it." She taps her fingers to her heart, a gesture she makes often. "Then it all went crazy."

We're having a suitably adult conversation about all this when Helen's agent comes in with tea. She's been by Helen's side since they both started out as models. "I'm not allowed to go to the festival," she says. "I'm never allowed to watch. If Helen's having her photo taken, I have to turn round and not look at her, because I make her laugh." Helen says: "We're too close. I can't have my family there, either, nor my boyfriend. I don't think he's ever met my alter ego. I wipe the facade off quite literally when I come home. I collapse on the sofa and get the Wet Wipes out." When her agent has left the room again, she adds, "I couldn't be in this industry without her. Trying to find a balance of normality – that's what I personally need. She's taught me everything. She always says that to be humble is to be sane."

TIP STRIP

Question 31: Look for the words *at first* in the first paragraph – the answer follows this.

Question 33: Look for words that match the adjectives in the options.

Question 34: Read what Helen does for the BFC.

31 According to the writer, at first glance the real Helen Blakemore appears

- **A** incredibly tall.
- **B** strikingly unusual.
- **C** extremely attractive.
- **D** surprisingly ordinary.

32 How did Helen react to the writer's first comment?

- **A** She revealed her embarrassment.
- **B** She kept her feelings to herself.
- **C** She accepted the compliment.
- **D** She showed her amusement.

33 What did the writer realise about Helen from a TV documentary?

- **A** how uncompetitive she is
- **B** how easily hurt she is
- **C** how shy she really is
- **D** how sensible she is

34 In the third paragraph, we learn that Helen

- **A** helps girls to find work as models.
- **B** gives regular interviews to the press.
- **C** is involved in providing talented people with funds.
- **D** organises support for models with personal problems.

35 As a schoolgirl, Helen

- **A** did some training that was later to prove useful.
- **B** overcame feelings of self-consciousness about her height.
- **C** was not studying with a view to following any particular career.
- **D** decided to change her appearance in order to get herself noticed.

36 In the final paragraph, we learn that Helen

- **A** finds it impossible to keep her work and private life separate.
- **B** feels like a different person when she's working.
- **C** gets nervous if her agent watches her at work.
- **D** finds her work increasingly demanding.

Part 6

You are going to read four extracts from four articles in which college tutors give their views on social media. For questions **37 – 40**, choose from the extracts **A – D**. The reviewers may be chosen more than once.

In the exam, you mark your answers **on a separate answer sheet**.

A Dennis Freeman

College students are almost universally regular users of social media. These students claim to welcome the freedom it gives them to say stupid things or post ugly, unattractive or indeed unflattering pictures for others in their circle to see, and it also gives them an easy opportunity to be negative or even nasty if they so wish. Social interaction via the internet, albeit very largely trivial in nature, is so ubiquitous that it now seems hard to recall how things were before it existed. At every stage in its development, commentators have seriously underestimated both the extent to which the spread of social media would change people's lives and the sheer power of the internet to become the dominant means of communication. What's more, the appeal looks to set to grow irrespective of how superficial or ephemeral the latest apps or social media platforms might seem to be.

B Alison Alder

My students frequently express concerns about the power of social media and the harm it can unleash. They see it as perpetuating crazy conspiracy theories and providing an easy platform from which vicious attacks on essentially harmless individuals can be launched with impunity. But, if they're so concerned, why don't they just retreat from the latest platform by switching off, or deleting the latest social-media app? The alarming reality is that, for many of them, the use of social media and the devices which access it are something close to an addiction – a dependence maintained by the absolute centrality of social media and the internet more generally in their lives, as a means of communication and a source of news and ideas. Truth be told, nobody saw this coming as a phenomenon, save perhaps the software companies themselves, the sole aim of whose marketing departments was ensuring that their users remained hooked in.

C Rachel Bruno

Although nearly all college students willingly use social media, there hasn't been sufficient research to date to explain how providers succeeded in making their platforms and apps indispensable to users, even when they come to dominate an individual's life to the point of harm. Nobody has yet sought to measure the resulting collateral damage to more traditional forms of relationship and interaction, or to physical well-being. One exception to this is the disturbance to sleep patterns which has been shown to result from the irresistible urge to check devices through the night. What's remarkable is that some of these downsides were identified from the early days of the internet, but rather than prompting a pause for reflection on how these challenges might best be accommodated, they were pushed to one side as manifestations of technophobic conservatism. It remains to be seen whether the inherent worth of social media will someday be re-evaluated.

D Pat Jamieson

Having failed to foresee the emergence of social media, the attention of academic research has tended to focus on the generation of digital natives now reaching collage age, and the perception that social media use is habit forming and that this is the result of clever marketing and even cleverer design of platforms and apps. Whether or not an individual can become addicted to hand-held devices or the allure of the latest photo upload and sharing sites is surely questionable. What's more, making the comparison with true addictions seems distinctly superficial unless backed up by further study. However, the near-universal engagement with social media amongst this particular demographic can't be denied, and has implications for the future, especially given the ongoing development of increasingly creative and relevant platforms and apps, capable of engaging our interest as well as performing a vital function in underpinning social interactions.

Which tutor

has a different opinion to Dennis Freeman regarding the extent to which the impact of social media was predicted? 37

shares Alison Alder's view about why people continue to use social media? 38

has a different view to the others regarding the attitude of college students to social media? 39

has a different view to Pat Jamieson about the lasting value of social-media platforms and apps? 40

Part 7

You are going to read an article about a travel book. Six paragraphs have been removed from the article. Choose from the paragraphs **A – G** the one which fits each gap (**41 – 46**). There is one extra paragraph which you do not need to use.

In the exam, you mark your answers **on a separate answer sheet**.

The long way home

On the last day, I walked down to the harbour. Having slept late, I had breakfast on my own and, as Charley was still sleeping, went for a wander. I wanted to get to the ocean; I needed to see the Pacific. I stumbled down the hill, through rows and rows of tenements, nodding, smiling and waving at the people I passed, eventually arriving at the waterfront. I turned round and lifted my camera to my eye and took a photograph.

| 41 |

I walked on. The path led to the beach. Although it was the last day of June, it was the first day the sun had shone in Magadan that year. Three weeks earlier, it had snowed. But that day, the air was warm and soft, the sky a cloudless blue. Women wore bikinis and small children were running naked across the sands. Families were eating picnics or cooking on barbecues. I walked past them all, along the entire length of the beach, until I came to the harbour.

| 42 |

All we knew then was that we wanted to get from London to Magadan. With the maps laid out in front of us, Charley and I drew a route, arbitrarily assigning mileage to each day, not knowing anything about the state of the roads. Time and again we were told by experienced travellers that our plans were wildly optimistic and that we didn't know what we were letting ourselves in for. I'd never ridden off-road and Charley had never properly camped. The chances of failure were high, they said.

| 43 |

I thought back to the day a month or so earlier when we had been in Mongolia. It was mid-afternoon and we were riding through a beautiful valley. I pulled over and got off my bike. Charley, ahead of me, stopped, too. He swung his bike around and rode back towards me. Before he even arrived, I could feel it coming off him: why are we stopping? We're not getting petrol, we're not stopping to eat: why are we stopping?

| 44 |

It was where we were going to stop at in the middle of an afternoon so that we could cool our sweaty feet in the water while catching fish that we'd cook that evening on an open fire under a star-speckled sky. I'd seen that spot half an hour earlier. There was no question at all that it was the one. A beautiful expanse of water and nobody for hundreds of miles. And we'd ridden straight past it.

| 45 |

Then we got back on our bikes and moved on. A few weeks later, we arrived at the first big river in Siberia. It was too wide, too fast and too deep to cross on a motorbike. There was a bridge, but it had collapsed.

| 46 |

I understood now that it didn't really matter that we hadn't stopped beside that cool, fast-flowing Mongolian river. The imperfections in our journey were what made it perfect. And maybe we wouldn't be in Magadan now if we'd not had that burning desire to keep going. After all, the river would always be there. Now that I knew what was out there, I could always return.

A Yet here we were in Magadan, as far around the globe from home as it was possible to go, and we'd arrived one day ahead of our schedule.

B We then guessed our way from west to east, across two continents, from the Atlantic to the Pacific, as far as it was possible to ride a motorbike in a straightish line.

C I walked away from Charley. I didn't want to tell him it was because we'd passed the place. The place that had been in my dreams. The place we'd fantasised about months before we'd even set off from London. A place with a river of cool, white water and a field nearby to pitch our tents.

D There it was: Magadan, Siberia. The place that had been in my dreams and thoughts for two years, like a mythical city forever beyond my reach. I wanted to capture it, somehow hold on to it, take a part of it with me when Charley and I began the long journey back.

E I thought Charley would be itching to get ahead, impatient with the hold-up. But he was in his element. He knew that someone or something would be along to help. The delays were the journey. We'd get across it when we got across it.

F I sat down for five minutes, just needing to look at the countryside around us. The countryside that we often didn't have time to take in because we were always so intent on keeping to our schedule.

G There, I climbed up on to the quay and sat on a mushroom-shaped bollard. An Alsatian came over and sat next to me. I scratched its head for a while, gazed out at the ocean and thought back to the day when Charley and I had sat in a little workshop in west London, surrounded by motorbikes, with dreams of the open road in our heads.

Part 8

You are going to read an article in which restaurant owners talk about raising money for charity. For questions **47 – 56**, choose from the sections (**A – D**). The sections may be chosen more than once.

In the exam, mark your answers **on a separate answer sheet**.

Which restaurant owner mentions

feeling uncomfortable about the inequalities that exist in the world?	47
a disappointing response to an attempt to raise awareness?	48
a reason for choosing this charity over others?	49
long-term projects organised by the charity?	50
activities aimed at increasing the amount individuals give?	51
a feeling of goodwill towards participating restaurants?	52
the need for more restaurants to get involved?	53
the need for customers to be aware that they are donating?	54
how much of the money collected reaches the people in need?	55
a commercial benefit of taking part in the project?	56

TIP STRIP

Question 47: Look for the owner who talks about the problem of hunger in the world.

Question 50: Look for references to the future in the option.

Question 51: Look for a word that expresses a similar idea to the verb *to give*.

Charity begins at the dinner table

Restaurants all over Britain have raised £100,000 to fight hunger in the Third World. We spoke to the owners of participating restaurants.

A

As a business, we weren't looking for a charity to support, but when we heard about this one, we just knew it was right for us. The campaign is making a real difference in the daily fight against hunger, and it's not just a question of saving the lives of severely malnourished children when there's a crisis, though that happens, it's also about helping to enable people in over 40 countries to feed themselves and their families in the future. That way hunger can be kept at bay and crises averted. The aim at the moment is to bring as many restaurants on board as possible, because by coming together, the catering community can make a real impact. Each customer giving a small donation, each manager or chef putting together a local fund-raising event, it all contributes enormously to the fight against hunger. And the charity makes sure that a high percentage of the funds collected actually find their way to the people who need it most.

B

The charity is particularly important for people in this profession. What we do is essentially superficial and frivolous and it makes me uneasy at times to think that while people here are spending lavishly on slap-up meals, people elsewhere are going hungry. We simply put a surcharge on every customer's bill, openly of course because they need to appreciate what they are a part of. Most people co-operate willingly, but anyone who feels strongly can ask to have the donation removed, though, of course, it's disappointing when that happens. It's important to celebrate the food we have, and we're not in the business of making our customers feel guilty about the relative plenty they enjoy, but at the same time we should be mindful of people less fortunate than ourselves. We're also organising a gala dinner where well-known TV celebrities will be putting in an appearance. Tickets for that will be at a premium, and the restaurant will be doing the dinners at cost.

C

We've been targeted by a whole raft of charities in recent years, but this one stood out for me as a very relevant choice for a restaurant business. Although customers don't generally object to a donation being added to their bill, we've found that actually engaging their interest leads to enhanced donations. Competitions such as guessing the weight of a cake, local TV celebrities serving at table, demonstrations by the head chef, etc., all these things bring people into the restaurant during the week of the appeal and create a festive atmosphere, even if they are mostly regular customers. We don't set out to increase trade through our charity work, although I would hope that customers will feel well disposed to establishments that show they have a conscience.

D

For us, the charity week came just when we needed something to give us a boost. We've only recently taken over the restaurant from a manager who'd been involved with various local fund-raising initiatives. But increased competition had eaten into his profitability and he'd decided to sell up. We knew, therefore, that there was an existing client base out there, who had been generous in the past, and we were looking for a way of raising our profile. We leafleted local businesses, colleges and libraries with details of the charity's work and our involvement with it. Although relatively few people came in during the week, which was a bit of a setback for us, the write-up in the local press did wonders in terms of spreading the word that we were here. So we took a long-term view and thought it was worth having another go this year. We've been working on a booklet of recipes which we'll give customers in return for a donation next time, which will also highlight local produce and recipes.

GUIDANCE: WRITING

Testing focus

Part 1
The focus of assessment in Part 1 is on dealing with given information so that you can present a coherent and logical argument in your essay. You must include two of the three points raised in the task. Marks are awarded for suitable content, good organisation, a wide range of language and communicative achievement. You should use a register appropriate for an essay.

Part 2
The focus of assessment in Part 2 is on writing appropriately, coherently and on answering the question. You should use an appropriate organisation and layout for the given task. Marks are awarded for suitable content, organisation (including coherence and cohesion, which might include using appropriate linking words) and communicative achievement. You should also use a range of language (vocabulary and structures) in the right register for the given task.

Preparation

General points
- Practise writing tasks in the given time. There is no point in spending longer than 45 minutes when writing a practice task. In the exam, each task carries equal marks, so there's nothing to gain by spending too long on Part 1 and then not having enough time to complete Part 2.
- Practise writing only the required number of words. There's no point in writing answers that are too long as they may take too much time and include irrelevant information.
- Work with a partner and edit one another's work so that you can help each other identify recurring mistakes. Keep a checklist of your own grammatical and spelling mistakes so that you know what to look out for in the exam.
- Get into the habit of reading the instructions carefully every time you answer a question, and always check your writing to make sure that you have included everything required.
- Check that you understand the appropriate format and register for every task type found in the exam.
- Revise connectors so you can use these appropriately in any task.
- Always read your work through to check that it's coherent and makes sense. Don't only check for grammar or spelling mistakes.

Part 1
- Read all the notes and opinions before you start to write.
- Practise ways of presenting evidence to support your opinions.
- Keep a note of discussions in class or articles you've read on different general topics as these may help to give you ideas for your essay.

Part 2
- Spend time thinking of issues and ideas for different topics so that you have ideas for the different tasks. You could build up a file with these ideas and refer to it when you practise writing a task or revise for the exam.
- Consider what your own strengths in writing are. Do you like writing lively and interesting answers, or more formal and informative answers? This will help you choose the best type of task in the exam.
- The questions in the exam may require you to use different language functions. Work on different ways of saying things such as giving advice, describing, explaining and so on.

Part 1

You must answer this question. Write your answer in **220 – 260** words in an appropriate style. In the exam, you write your answer **on a separate answer sheet**.

1 You have had a class discussion on ways technology has improved or spoiled the quality of our lives. You have made the notes below:

> **Technology in our lives**
> - communicating easily
> - ways of learning
> - filling free time

> Some opinions expressed in the discussion:
>
> "Sometimes I wish people would stop texting me!"
>
> "Life was so much better in the past – it was easier to learn in school with books."
>
> "I think that playing video games and watching TV are a waste of time."

Write an essay discussing **two** of the ways in your notes in which technology affects our lives. You should **explain which way you think has had the greatest positive or negative impact** on our lives, **giving reasons** to support your opinion.

You may, if you wish, make use of the opinions expressed in the discussion, but you should use your own words as far as possible.

TIP STRIP

An essay should be written in a semi-formal or formal style. Read all the input and choose which two aspects of technology you want to discuss. Think about reasons for and against each aspect of technology, with examples to support your ideas.

- Decide which of your two points has had the greatest positive or negative impact on people's lives, and why. You can balance your points but make sure your line of argument and examples support your conclusion.
- Remember to include an introduction to the topic of technology in everyday life in general before you start discussing specific ideas.
- You don't have to use the opinions given – you may have plenty of ideas of your own. If you do use the ideas given, don't use the exact same words, just use the ideas.
- Link your ideas clearly and coherently using a range of connectors and clear paragraphs.
- Use a range of language to explain and justify the points you want to make.
- Make your argument as interesting and persuasive as possible.

WRITING **TEST 2**

Part 2

Write an answer to **one** of the questions **2 – 4** in this part. Write your answer in **220 – 260** words in an appropriate style. In the exam, you write your answer **on a separate answer sheet**, and put the question number in the box at the top of the page.

2   You have received an email from an English friend:

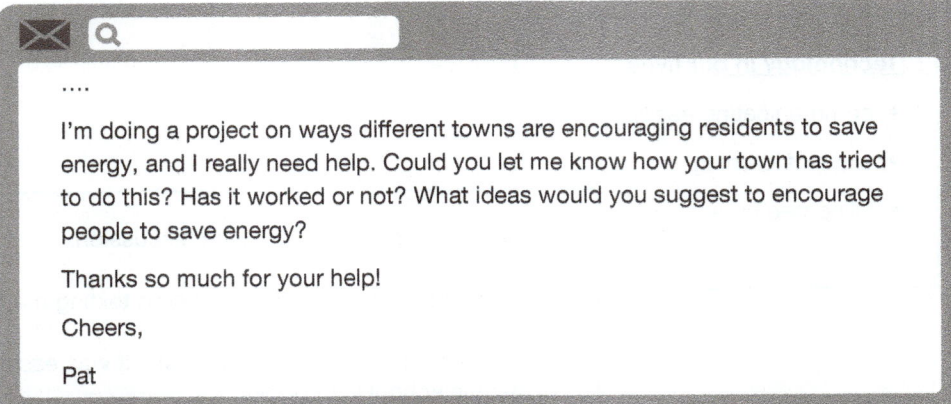

….

I'm doing a project on ways different towns are encouraging residents to save energy, and I really need help. Could you let me know how your town has tried to do this? Has it worked or not? What ideas would you suggest to encourage people to save energy?

Thanks so much for your help!

Cheers,

Pat

Write your **email**.

3   Your college wants to help new students settle in to college life easily.
The principal has asked the Social committee to write a report outlining what is currently done to help new students, identifying things that need improving and making recommendations for how these improvements could be implemented.

Write your **report**.

4   You see this announcement on a film website:

Good or bad?

We're compiling a list of what films fans think are the five best and worst films of the last decade.

Send us a review of your nomination of the best or worst film you've seen in the last decade, and we'll consider it. The best reviews will be posted on the website with the completed list.

Write your **review**.

TIP STRIP

Question 2:
In an informal email you should use informal language, link your ideas with connectors and organise your answer clearly and logically.

Question 3:
A report is often written for someone in authority, in a formal or semi-formal style.
- Provide extra details if appropriate but don't include things that are not relevant.
- Outline the current situation for students, identify areas for improving and make recommendations for implementing changes.
- Possible headings could be: 'Current Situation', 'What needs improving', 'Recommendations', and 'Conclusion'.

Question 4:
Reviews should interest and engage the reader. Write an engaging opening. Organise it clearly, with paragraphs, ending with your opinion.

GUIDANCE: LISTENING

Testing focus

Part 1
There is a range of testing focuses in Part 1 questions.
- Some questions focus on a detailed understanding of parts of the recording, or on the use of particular vocabulary or expressions.
- Some questions test your understanding of the recording as a whole, or of the speakers' attitudes, feelings or opinions.
- Some questions test your understanding of the interaction between the two speakers, e.g. of whether they are in agreement.

Part 2
Part 2 tests your ability to locate, understand and record specific information from the recording.
- This task doesn't test grammar, so you don't have to change the form of the words you hear. However, you should check the grammar of the sentence to check if the word you've heard is, for example, singular or plural.
- This task doesn't test extra information. If you write too much, you risk losing the mark by not creating a good sentence.

Part 3
Part 3 tests a detailed understanding of the speakers' feelings, attitudes and opinions. Each question relates to a specific section of text and there is a range of testing focus.
- Some questions focus on a single phrase or sentence in the recording.
- Some questions ask you to interpret the meaning of a whole long turn from one speaker.
- Some questions test your understanding of interaction between two of the speakers.

Part 4
Part 4 is designed to test your understanding of what people say, as well as the ability to pick out key words and phrases.
Each of the two tasks has a separate focus and you need to listen for two separate ideas. For example, getting the right answer for a speaker in Task One doesn't help you to get the right answer for that speaker in Task Two.

Preparation

- Remember that the Cambridge Advanced exam aims to test real-life skills, so any listening practice you do is likely to improve your general listening skills.
- Get used to listening to a range of people speaking in English. In the exam, you need to understand people of different ages, people from different social backgrounds and people speaking in both formal and informal situations.
- Practise listening to a range of accents in English. In the exam you can expect to hear people with different accents, e.g. British, American, Australian, etc.
- Search online for an English-language radio programme, podcast or video clip that interests you. Listen and try to note down the key ideas you hear.
- Watch English-language films and video clips with the English subtitles on. Concentrate on connecting what you hear with what you read in the subtitles. Watch the clip again with the subtitles turned off. This time you'll already have an idea of what's being said, and can really focus on what you hear.
- When you're doing practice tests, pay attention to the type of language used in the questions. For example, you can expect to see ideas summarised using abstract nouns and reporting verbs in the questions. You need to match these ideas with the more conversational language you hear on the recording. Make sure you're familiar with how ideas and expressions in spoken language are reported more succinctly in written language. This will help you in the Listening test.

Part 1

You will hear three different extracts. For questions **1 – 6** choose the answer (**A**, **B**, or **C**) which fits best according to what you hear. There are two questions for each extract.

In the exam, write your answers **on a separate answer sheet**.

Extract One

You hear two people on a music programme talking about a new album by a band called Sharpie.

1 What is the woman's opinion of the band's new album?

    A   She finds it generally uninspiring.
    B   She thinks that their last one was better.
    C   She feels it may not enjoy great success.

2 What do the two speakers agree about?

    A   the quality of the song writing
    B   the inadequacy of the sleeve notes
    C   the effectiveness of the marketing campaign

Extract Two

You overhear two students talking about a design course they are following.

3 What do they feel about the word 'sophisticated'?

    A   Their lecturer uses it more than most design people.
    B   It's been used so much that it has lost its meaning.
    C   Design textbooks should define it more precisely.

4 The man mentions some Italian furniture as an example of something which

    A   is much less complicated in design than it appears.
    B   gives an overall impression of something that is stylish.
    C   reflects the desire of some designers to go against the trend.

TIP STRIP

Question 2: The woman says: *I know what you mean.* What is she referring to?

Question 4: He's giving an example of what the woman has just said.

Question 5: Listen for an expression that means 'looking back'.

Extract Three

You hear part of an interview with a man who has recently given up his city job to go and live in the country.

5 Looking back, how does he feel about his earlier attempts at self-sufficiency?

    A   He regrets the mistakes he made.
    B   He accepts that he was rather idealistic.
    C   He feels bitter about having to give it up.

6 He admits that in his new home, he won't be

    A   as reliant on making an income from the land.
    B   so worried about living in an environmentally friendly way.
    C   attempting the same range of activities as he did previously.

Part 2

You will hear part of a podcast about how offices may be designed to suit different types of workers in the future. For questions 7 – 14, complete the sentences with a word or short phrase.

In the exam, mark your answers **on a separate answer sheet**.

THE OFFICE OF THE FUTURE

What's called the (7) .... office is given as an example of one prediction that hasn't come true.

Francis Duffy, an (8) .... by profession, identifies four types of office.

Duffy gives the name 'the hive' to the type of office where work of a (9) .... nature is carried out.

'The cell' is a type of office which suits people whose work requires (10) ....

Duffy thinks that people such as computer scientists and (11) .... work well in a cell office.

The type of office which Duffy calls 'the den' was designed to make (12) .... easier.

Duffy sees people involved in professions like (13) .... and the media working well in a den office.

Duffy says 'clubs' are the type of office which would suit people doing what he calls (14) .... work.

TIP STRIP

Question 7: Listen for another way of saying 'called' – the answer follows this.

Question 9: A hive is where bees live – what are bees like by nature? Listen to check.

Question 13: Remember to read the words after the gap – you're listening for another profession not mentioned in the sentence.

Part 3

You will hear an interview with two underwater photographers called Alex Mustard, and Nina Hanna, who have just published a successful book featuring their work.
For questions **15 – 20**, choose the answer (**A, B, C** or **D**) which fits best according to what you hear.

15 What does Alex say about filming wildlife underwater?

   A   It's impossible to plan what you'll see.
   B   It's fairly easy to set up controlled shots.
   C   You have to work closely with other people.
   D   You have to be quick to exploit opportunities.

16 When she was photographing free-diving, Nina

   A   found it hard to capture the point of the sport.
   B   didn't really go deep enough to get good shots.
   C   came to admire what the divers were able to do.
   D   wanted to keep her own feelings out of the images.

17 What does Alex say about his favourite shots in the book?

   A   They are the ones he had most fun shooting.
   B   It was hard to get the divers to take them seriously.
   C   They may embarrass some of the divers who feature in them.
   D   It's unusual to see shots that show the light-hearted side of diving.

18 How does Nina feel about photographing dangerous creatures underwater?

   A   She tries to avoid looking aggressive in their company.
   B   She dislikes the idea of disturbing them in any way.
   C   She recognises the need to avoid certain species.
   D   She can tell if an animal is likely to attack her.

19 Alex agrees with Nina that anyone wanting to take up underwater photography should

   A   choose subjects that are likely to keep relatively still.
   B   buy the most expensive equipment they can.
   C   avoid getting too close to their subjects.
   D   take shots of small things at first.

20 For Alex, the main attraction of going to Sardinia is

   A   the number of submerged wrecks he can explore.
   B   the convenient location of the main dive sites.
   C   the range of underwater life that he can see.
   D   the temperature and clarity of the water.

TIP STRIP

Question 15: Listen to Alex's first answer. The first part of what he says is about wildlife.

Question 17: Listen for the word *favourite* in the interviewer's question and Alex's reply.

Question 19: Listen to what Nina says to find the answer.

LISTENING **TEST 2**

TEST 2

LISTENING

Part 4

You will hear five short extracts in which people who have recently changed their accommodation are talking about their experiences.

In the exam, mark your answers **on a separate answer sheet**.

TASK ONE

For questions **21 – 25**, choose from the list (**A – H**) the reason each speaker gives for deciding to change their accommodation.

A	relationships with others	
B	limited space	Speaker 1 [ ] **21**
C	poor physical environment	Speaker 2 [ ] **22**
D	flexible working practices	Speaker 3 [ ] **23**
E	employer's relocation	Speaker 4 [ ] **24**
F	time spent travelling	Speaker 5 [ ] **25**
G	rising cost of living	
H	a wish for independence	

While you listen you must complete both tasks.

TASK TWO

For questions **26 – 30**, choose from the list (**A – H**) the unexpected disadvantage of their accommodation each speaker mentions.

A	larger bills	
B	a feeling of isolation	Speaker 1 [ ] **26**
C	unreliable public transport	Speaker 2 [ ] **27**
D	dealing with difficult people	Speaker 3 [ ] **28**
E	a lack of leisure facilities	Speaker 4 [ ] **29**
F	poor local services	Speaker 5 [ ] **30**
G	an unhelpful owner	
H	bad neighbours	

TIP STRIP

Speaker 1: Listen to what the speaker says about college to find the answer to 21.
Speaker 4: Listen to what the speaker says about the landlord to get the answer to 29.
Speaker 5: Listen to what the speaker says about buses to get the answer to 30.

GUIDANCE: SPEAKING

Testing focus

General points
You're assessed on your own individual performance by the examiner and the interlocutor.
- The examiner uses descriptors from the assessment scales to assess your performance throughout the test and awards marks for the following criteria – grammatical and lexical resource, discourse management, pronunciation, and interactive communication.
- The interlocutor gives a global mark for achievement at the end of the test.
- It's important to remember that you're not assessed on your actual ideas, just on the language you use to express them. Don't worry if you feel you have nothing important to say – it's the language you use that counts!

Part 1
This focuses on general interactional language and social interaction. Try to be relaxed and answer the questions in an interesting way, but don't give too much detail.

Part 2
This focuses on organising a longer unit of discourse. You have to compare two pictures, then answer two questions by expressing opinions and speculating about them. Make sure you compare the pictures before you go on to speculate about them.

Part 3
The focus in this part is on interacting with your partner. You have to exchange ideas, give and justify opinions, agree and disagree, make suggestions, speculate, and evaluate different ideas. You also have to reach a decision by negotiating with your partner. You should listen carefully to what your partner says, and develop the discussion as much as possible. Try to use a range of language.

Part 4
The focus is on developing more abstract ideas with your partner by giving and justifying opinions, agreeing and disagreeing. Although you may each be asked individual questions, you can also develop your partner's ideas and contribute to a discussion of the question asked.

Revision tips

Part 1
- Although you shouldn't prepare whole speeches, you should practise talking about general topics in small groups or with your partner.
- Prepare questions to ask your partner on given topics, and take it in turns to ask and answer the questions.
- Practise this part for two minutes, so that you feel how long your answers should be.
- Practise using different tenses in your answers. For example, if you are asked what you like doing in the evenings, you could say that you used to play tennis but now you prefer to watch films.

Part 2
- Practise comparing pictures from newspapers, magazines or the internet. Focus on comparing, not describing, and think about different ways of expressing comparisons.
- When you practise specific exam tasks, work with a partner and try to find three things to say when you're comparing your two pictures and three things to say about the rest of the task. This technique will help you to organise your talk within the given time in the exam.
- Practise organising your talk by linking ideas using connectors, e.g. *whereas*, *conversely*. Build up a list of these connectors so that you can use them confidently.
- Practise on your own by looking at pictures and thinking of interesting things to say about them. You could write down key words and use them to organise your talk in a logical way.

Part 3
- Practise discussing exam tasks with a partner and time yourself in two minutes. This will help you to feel how long the time is. However, in the exam you shouldn't worry about timing yourself as the interlocutor will stop you after two minutes, so you can concentrate on your discussion and say everything you want to say.
- When you're asked to make a decision, listen carefully to the interlocutor's question and then discuss it in detail with your partner. Don't just point to the prompt you choose, or make your decision too quickly. Use the full minute for your negotiation.
- It doesn't matter if you run out of time before you have agreed on your decision as it is the language you use in the discussion that's important.
- Make sure you practise listening to your partner so that you can respond appropriately to what they say. It's good to refer to what they have said when you make a point, as this shows genuine interaction.
- Think about different ways of asking your partner for their opinion, and of agreeing and disagreeing with them, e.g. *that's interesting, but not exactly what I think*.
- It's important for you to initiate ideas as well as respond to what your partner says, so practise ways of doing that, e.g. *What do you think about …?*
- Practise using conversation 'fillers' to give yourself time to think if necessary, e.g. *let me think …*
- Keep a list of language functions such as interrupting politely, e.g. *may I make a point here*; moving a discussion on, e.g. *let's move on …*; and reacting to what your partner says, e.g. *really?* Use these appropriately in the exam.

Part 4
- Discuss issues in the news with classmates so you have ideas on different topics. You can also get ideas from the Cambridge Advanced Reading and Listening texts that you study in class. Keep a note of interesting ideas so that you can read them again before the exam in case that topic comes up.
- Remember you can disagree with your partner, and this is often very productive! Practise this by making statements for your partner to agree or disagree with.
- Remember that the examiners can only mark what they hear. Try to contribute to general discussions in class as much as possible so that you get used to expressing your opinions. Always speak clearly.

TEST 2 SPEAKING

Part 1 (2 minutes)

The examiner will ask you one or two questions about yourself and what you think about everyday topics such as work or study, travel, holidays, daily life and routines.
For example:

- Would you say you're an organised sort of person? (Why / Why not?)
- Have you always enjoyed the same kind of music? (Why / Why not?)
- How do you prefer to relax in the evenings during the week? (Why?)
- When you're on holiday, do you prefer sightseeing or taking it easy? (Why?)
- What would your perfect job be? (Why?)
- Do you have any ambitions for the near future? (Why / Why not?)
- Do you prefer watching, or playing sport? (Why?)
- Would you like to live and work in another country in future? (Why / Why not?)

Part 2 (4 minutes)

CELEBRATING SOMETHING SPECIAL

Turn to the pictures on page 173. They show people celebrating something special.

(Candidate A): I'd like you to compare **two** of the pictures, and say **why the celebration might be special to the people, and how memorable it might be**.

(Candidate B), **who do you think will get the greatest pleasure from the celebration?**

PLAYING MUSIC

Turn to the pictures on page 174. They show people playing music in different situations.

(Candidate B), compare **two** of the pictures, and say **how easy it might be to play music in these situations, and how important it might be to practise regularly**.

(Candidate A), **who do you think might need the most practice? (Why?)**

TIP STRIP

Part 1:

Make your answers interesting, but not too long. You shouldn't answer your partner's questions in this part nor add anything to what they have said. For the first four questions you answer:
I'm not organised in my social life, because I like to be spontaneous, but I am very organised in my studies.
I think my tastes in music have changed. When I was younger I loved pop music, but now I'm a bit more sophisticated and I like jazz. Maybe because my father enjoys it and enjoy it together.
I don't have much time to relax during the week because I have homework. I like to read before I go to sleep or watch the news on television because I like to keep up with what's happening.
I love sightseeing. I hate lying on a beach somewhere. I want to discover places.

Part 2:

Remember that there are three things to do: compare the pictures and answer two further questions. You should use language of speculation: *it's possible that ...*, etc.

Celebrating something special

Candidate A, you could say: *The woman who's just had a baby looks so happy. Maybe it's her first child so it must be very special ... The sports team have obviously just won a trophy, and perhaps it's the first one they've won for a long time. That's why they'll remember the moment because there will be photos and media interviews ... The woman will certainly remember the celebration because she'll have to bring the baby up.*

Playing music

Candidate B, you could say: *The boy may be just starting to learn how to play, so possibly it's his father who is teaching him. That's quite stressful because he undoubtedly wants to impress his father. He has to practise a lot. The buskers don't look stressed at all – they could be just having fun, and so they don't need to practise much, although if they want to make some money, they have to be good.*

Part 3 (4 minutes)

Now I'd like you to talk together for about two minutes.

Here are some areas in which people think it's necessary to keep up with developments. First you have some time to look at the task. *[Turn to the task on page 175]*

Now talk to each other about **how necessary it is for people to keep in touch with developments in these areas**.

Thank you.

Now you have a minute to decide **in which area it is most important for people to keep in touch with developments**.

Part 4 (5 minutes)

Answer these questions.

- Some people don't like any kind of change. Why do you think they feel like this?
- Do you think it's better to know a little about many things or a lot about one thing? (Why?)
- Do you think that some people are too concerned with appearance nowadays? (Why / Why not?)
- Do you think everything changes too quickly nowadays? (Why / Why not?)
- Some people say that people become dissatisfied with what they have too easily. Do you agree?
- In your opinion, do people generally have the right priorities in life? (Why / Why not?)

Select any of the following prompts, as appropriate:
- What do you think?
- Do you agree?
- How about you?

TIP STRIP

Part 3:
Focus your discussion on the prompts, and consider how important it is for people to keep in touch with developments in these areas. This means assessing their importance individually. It doesn't matter whether you talk about them all. It's more important to use a range of language. You could say: Fashion's important for people who are worried about their image, but it changes quickly. It's important to know what's happening in technology because otherwise you can't use the latest software. It's important to update everything regularly, although it's expensive. Initiate discussion and ask for your partner's opinion: You said it's crucial to know about the latest work opportunities, and I agree, but what about social media? What makes you think that?

TIP STRIP

Part 4:
This is a discussion, and you can add to your partner's ideas. The general topic here is change, and how people deal with it. You could talk about:
- not wanting to take chances; being afraid to try something new
- knowing a little about many things makes you look clever, but you may not be efficient at doing anything
- problems with media influence; fascination with celebrities; wanting to look good; not valuing personality over looks
- in the world of technology things change quickly; the media reports everything immediately; it's a society where people want everything now and won't wait
- things you have to work hard for are more satisfying; society is rather superficial so people move on quickly
- health; family/relationships; some people think money can buy everything but it can't

TEST 3

Part 1

For questions **1 – 8**, read the text below and decide which answer (**A**, **B**, **C** or **D**) best fits each gap. There is an example at the beginning (**0**).

In the exam, you mark your answers **on a separate answer sheet**.

Example:

0   A remind   B memorise   C remember   D commemorate

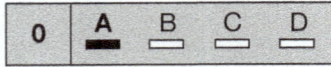

What makes a good souvenir?

On my desk I have a collection of souvenirs; objects that **(0)** .... me of places I've visited and important events in my life. There's a model boat that I saw being **(1)** .... from a piece of wood on a Caribbean island, a piece of lava that **(2)** .... hot from a volcano in the year I was born, and a shell **(3)** .... on my favourite childhood beach.

It's as if the longer you hold on to certain objects, the **(4)** .... their associations with the past become and the sharper the recollections that gather around them. They are, **(5)** .... , real souvenirs, encapsulations not only of the place, but also of your time in the place. But these days, the term 'real souvenirs' sounds like a contradiction in **(6)** .... and this is because the objects sold to tourists as souvenirs are often cheap mass-produced imports that have nothing to **(7)** .... with the place at all. By buying something made by local people using sustainable local materials, however, you're effectively **(8)** .... to the local economy.

1	A sketched	B carved	C thrown	D scratched
2	A developed	B appeared	C emerged	D arrived
3	A found out	B bumped into	C come across	D picked up
4	A wider	B greater	C larger	D harder
5	A albeit	B otherwise	C whereas	D therefore
6	A terms	B meanings	C words	D names
7	A gain	B do	C make	D get
8	A contributing	B supporting	C encouraging	D sustaining

Part 2

For questions **9 – 16**, read the text below and think of the word which best fits each gap. Use only **one** word in each gap. There is an example at the beginning (**0**).

In the exam, you write your answers **IN CAPITAL LETTERS on a separate answer sheet**.

Example: **0** H A S

Sushi chef

Kazutoshi Endo **(0)** .... been making the Japanese fish and rice delicacy known as sushi for 13 years. Yet he wants to **(9)** .... it clear that he's still **(10)** .... much a beginner. In fact, he's quite adamant about it, **(11)** .... being head sushi chef at one of London's leading Japanese restaurants.

Endo comes from a hard-working family in the port city of Yokohama and is a third-generation sushi chef. Although he trained to be a sports teacher, it was always Endo's ambition to follow in his father's footsteps. He was never taught **(12)** .... to do though, because the **(13)** .... you learn in Japan is to watch the experts. Some chefs spend three years washing sushi rice, in order to observe the masters at work.

And it takes some concentration to keep your eye on Endo's hands as he makes sushi. All it takes is just a **(14)** .... quick cuts with his knife and a neat pile of perfectly sliced octopus sits on the counter. A sushi roll may look **(15)** .... a simple rice dish, but apparently it takes years to learn how to roll rice **(16)** .... exactly the right amount of pressure. As Endo says: "Sushi has to be mastered. I can't explain the process in words."

Part 3

For questions **17 – 24**, read the text below. Use the word given in capitals at the end of some of the lines to form a word that fits in the gap **in the same line**. There is an example at the beginning (**0**).

In the exam, you write your answers **IN CAPITAL LETTERS on a separate answer sheet**.

Example: | 0 | H | I | G | H | L | I | G | H | T | S | | | | |

Creating the perfect CV

A great CV which **(0)** .... your skills and experience will boost your chances of getting a job interview. On average, a recruiter will spend just eight seconds reviewing each CV, so it's important to present the information in a clear, concise and **(17)** .... way.

LIGHT

PERSUADE

Your CV should look clean and tidy with no frills or fancy **(18)** .... , with all the information clearly signposted, and shouldn't exceed two pages. Include your name, address and contact details, but information about your **(19)** .... , age and hobbies isn't essential.

ATTACH

NATIONAL

Any **(20)** .... employer will be interested in your work experience. List the most recent first, describing your previous jobs in short sentences using straightforward, positive language which emphasies all your key **(21)** .... Similarly, list brief details of your academic and professional **(22)** .... along with the grades attained. Include specific skills such as languages and state your level. **(23)** .... looking for their first job are **(24)** .... to have much relevant work experience, so should stress their academic record and key skills.

PROSPECT

ACHIEVE
QUALIFY
APPLY
LIKE

Part 4

For questions **25 – 30**, complete the second sentence so that it has a similar meaning to the first sentence, using the word given. **Do not change the word given.** You must use between **three** and **six** words, including the word given. Here is an example (**0**).

Example:

0   Trevor persuaded his sister to enter the competition.

   TALKED

   Trevor .... entering the competition.

The gap can be filled with the words 'talked his sister into', so you write:

Example: | 0 | *TALKED HIS SISTER INTO*

In the exam, you write **only** the missing words **IN CAPITAL LETTERS** on a separate answer sheet.

---

25   We'd have run out of petrol if you hadn't called in at that service station.

   JUST

   It was .... in at that service station, or we'd have run out of petrol.

26   My cousins' unexpected visit enabled me to get out of doing my homework.

   PROVIDED

   My cousins' unexpected visit .... perfect excuse for not doing my homework.

27   Nobody can predict the real consequences of global warming.

   SAYING

   There's .... real consequences of global warming will be.

28   The football club is now being run by an experienced accountant.

   TAKEN

   An experienced accountant .... running of the football club.

29   People say that the celebrities will arrive in the next 30 minutes.

   EXPECTED

   The arrival .... in the next 30 minutes.

30   Some loss of support for the government is a likely consequence of these drastic measures.

   RESULT

   These drastic measures are .... the government losing some support.

Part 5

You are going to read an article about an actress. For questions **31 – 36**, choose the answer (**A, B, C** or **D**) which you think fits best according to the text.

In the exam, you mark your answers **on a separate answer sheet.**

What price privacy?

Don't blame technology for threatening our privacy – it's the way the institutions choose to use it.

The most depressing moment of my day is first thing in the morning, when I download my overnight batch of emails and feeds. Without fail, it contains dozens of messages from people who, knowing my interest in the subject, write to me describing violations of their personal privacy. Throughout the day, the stream continues, each message warning of yet another nail in the coffin of personal privacy. In other centuries, such invasions of liberty would have arisen from religious persecution or the activities of tax collectors. Nowadays, the invasions take place through the use of information technology.

So, when those of us who value personal privacy are asked for their view, we will invariably speak in disparaging terms about such technologies. In an effort to stem the speed and force of the invasion, we will sometimes argue that the technologies themselves should simply be banned. "Just stop using the cursed technology," we cry, "then there won't be any privacy issues." Of course, things aren't so simple. Even the strongest advocate of privacy recognises that technology can offer enormous benefits to individuals and to society. To prohibit a technology on the grounds that it's being used to invade privacy would also be to deny society the benefits of innovation.

The sensible perspective is that technology doesn't necessarily have to invade privacy. The reality is that it invariably does. Companies may well argue that customers are prepared to 'trade off' a little privacy in return for better service or a cooler and more sophisticated product. They say that this is a matter of free choice. I doubt that there's any genuine free choice in the matter. Whether I go with Orange or Vodaphone is indeed a free choice. But I have no choice over whether my communications data will or will not be stored by my communications provider. They know the location of my mobile and the numbers from which I received calls, and the emails I send are routinely stored by all providers, whether I like it or not.

CCTV also gives me no free choice. Its purpose may be to keep me secure, but I have no alternative but to accept it. Visual surveillance is becoming a fixed component in the design of modern urban centres, new housing areas, public buildings and increasingly throughout the road system. People now expect security cameras to be part of all forms of architecture and design. Of course, there's another side to the coin, many technologies have brought benefits to the consumer with little or no cost to privacy. Encryption is one that springs to mind. Many of the most valuable innovations in banking and communications could never have been deployed without this technique.

The problem with privacy is not technology, but the institutions which make use of it. Governments are hungry for data, and will use their powers to force companies to collect, retain and yield personal information on their customers. In recent years, governments have managed to incorporate surveillance into almost every aspect of our finances, communication and lifestyle. Whilst acknowledging the importance of privacy as a fundamental right, they argue that surveillance is needed to maintain law and order and create economic efficiency. The right to privacy, it's always claimed, shouldn't be allowed to stand in the way of the wider public interest. This argument is sound in principle, but there seems to be little intellectual or analytical basis for its universal and unquestioned application. Technology doesn't have to be the enemy of privacy. But while governments insist on requiring surveillance, and while companies insist on amassing personal information about their customers, technology will continue to be seen as such.

31 From the first paragraph, we understand that the writer

   A resents receiving such distressing emails from people.
   B is surprised that people should contact him about privacy.
   C finds it hard to cope with the tone of the emails he receives.
   D is resigned to the fact that invasions of privacy are on the increase.

32 What view does the writer put forward in the second paragraph?

   A People should be willing to do without certain forms of technology.
   B It is a mistake to criticise people for the way they use technology.
   C It is unrealistic to deny people the benefits that technology can bring.
   D People shouldn't be allowed to use technologies that threaten privacy.

33 The writer feels that some companies

   A do not really give customers a say in issues related to privacy.
   B fail to recognise that their products may invade people's privacy.
   C underestimate the strength of their customers' feelings about privacy.
   D refuse to make compromises with customers concerned about privacy.

34 What point does the writer make about CCTV?

   A People no longer question how necessary it is.
   B People feel more secure the more widely it is used.
   C It ought to be a feature of all new building projects.
   D It would be difficult for society to function without it.

35 The writer gives encryption as an example of a technology which

   A brings only questionable benefits to society in general.
   B poses much less of a threat to privacy than others.
   C actually helps us to protect personal privacy.
   D is worth losing some personal privacy for.

36 In the fifth paragraph, the writer suggests that governments are

   A justified in denying the right of privacy to criminals.
   B mistaken in their view that surveillance prevents crime.
   C wrong to dismiss the individual's right to privacy so lightly.
   D unreasonable in their attitude towards civil-rights campaigners.

Part 6

You are going to read four reviews of a collection of essays on local history. For questions **37 – 40**, choose from the extracts **A – D**. The extracts may be chosen more than once.

In the exam, you mark your answers **on a separate answer sheet**.

A

It isn't often that one comes across a book by an amateur historian that's as painstakingly researched as Emma Mortock's account of her home area in the time of Ancient Rome. It's her good fortune to live in a village that's witnessed a series of exciting archaeological excavations in recent years, and the author's achievement is to have distilled information from a number of highly technical reports into a single narrative that manages to be both accessible and intriguing. Mortock never dwells on the detail and the pace of the narrative never flags, but this is hardly a dumbing down because Ms. Mortock resists the temptation to speculate unduly about the artifacts themselves, and doesn't seek to romanticise the lives of their owners. The interweaving of the author's own line drawings and photography is subtle and helpful; indeed I'd like to have seen more of this feature. This is a book that whets your appetite for the wider topic.

B

Emma Mortock doesn't fit the stereotype of the dry amateur historian. In her early 20s, lively and outspoken, she's on a mission to bring local history to life for local people. This book certainly manages to achieve that. Although rather lacking in archaeological precision and detail, it's a cracking good read for anyone who just wants the bare facts, plus a bit of imaginative colour. I'm not sure how much of the story of the local Romano-British families was based on archaeology and how much was made up, but it certainly paints a vivid picture of the period for those who haven't studied the history in detail. The author's even done her own drawings of some of the Roman artifacts that were found in her village and these are both enlightening and charmingly executed. The objects themselves are now housed in the British Museum in London.

C

I must admit that when I was given Emma Mortock's slim volume of local history to read, my heart sank. I imagined a fanciful account by a well-meaning layperson who happened to live near some important excavations. As it turned out, I couldn't have been more wrong. Emma is a recent history graduate who teaches the subject at the local school. She's obviously read widely and there are tantalising references to the reports written by archaeologists who worked on the digs themselves, although sadly their findings aren't discussed in any detail. Although this isn't the sort of book that you're meant to read from cover to cover, I never got bogged down in the local detail. I did, however, find the rather grainy photographs a bit disappointing and could have done without the somewhat approximate line drawings. Overall, however, I came away with a clearer idea about life in Roman Britain, and I'm grateful for that.

D

Local history enthusiasts will be grateful to Emma Mortock, who's obviously been through various dense archaeological reports with great patience and selected just those artifacts and findings that are likely to catch the imagination of the non-specialist. The result is an attractive little volume of local history that certainly paints a vivid picture of the ups and downs of life in the Roman garrison town that once graced the corner of England where Emma lives. Her sketches and snapshots are competent enough and give the reader insights into the kind of artifacts that have been unearthed locally. It's a shame, however, that the prose is so measured and traditional. It's hardly a style that's going to appeal to a younger readership. Emma Mortock is a local teacher, and deserves praise for producing an original little book about the area in which she lives and works.

Which reviewer

shares Reviewer D's view of how effectively the author has made use of original source material? 37

has a different view to Reviewer A regarding the attractiveness of the illustrations in the book? 38

has a different view from the others about how readable the book is? 39

shares Reviewer C's view about how seriously the writer has treated the subject? 40

Part 7

You are going to read an extract from a newspaper article. Six paragraphs have been removed from the article. Choose from the paragraphs **A – G** the one which fits each gap (**41 – 46**). There is one extra paragraph which you do not need to use.

In the exam, you mark your answers **on a separate answer sheet**.

Call of the wild

What can wild animals tell us about the way life should be lived? Well, take the example of the whitethroat. You could say that it's a rather drab little bird with a rather ordinary and tuneless little song. Or, on the contrary, you could say the whitethroat is a messenger of excitement and danger – a thrilling embodiment of life and risk and defiance of death.

41

Whitethroats, however, are mostly lurkers and skulkers. You'll usually find them well hidden in a nice thick, prickly hedge, their brown plumage picked out with the small vanity of, yes, a whitethroat. The male bird sings a jumble of notes thrown together any old how, a song that is generally described as 'scratchy'. A whitethroat is not normally a bird that hands out thrills to human observers. But all the same, it is a bird that lives by the thrill and is prepared to die by the thrill.

42

Or not, of course. A small bird that makes such a big racket and then flies into the open will clearly excite the interest of every bird of prey within earshot. And that is part of the point: "Come on, you hawks! Have a go if you think you're hard enough!"

43

But I can't help wondering how the bird feels about this. Does he do it because he is a clock, a feathered machine that has been wound up by the passing of the seasons to make this proven ancestral response? Or does he do it because making a springtime song flight is the most wonderfully thrilling thing to do?

44

And it is there in aspects of human behaviour too. I have spoken to mountaineers, power-boaters, Grand Prix drivers, parachutists and jockeys and they all say the same thing. It's not something they do because they have a death wish. The exact opposite is the case – risk makes them feel more intensely, more gloriously alive. They take risks because they love life. It is part of the contradiction of being ourselves. We thrill to danger. We can't resist it. We love safety and security and comfort, yet we seek risk and adventure.

45

That's why we watch films and identify with risk-taking heroes and feisty heroines in all kinds of precarious situations. It's why we pass the time on a long journey by reading a thriller in which the main character dodges death by inches all the way to our destination. And it explains why we support a football team; knowing that the more we care, the more we will find both excitement and despair.

46

But if home is so great, why did we ever leave it? And if adventure is so great, why did we come back? It is because our nature – our human, mammalian, animal nature – insists that we love both; that one is not complete without the other.

A And so, like the whitethroat, we all seek danger, even if we don't take the actual risks ourselves. In other words, although we've spent 99 per cent of that history as hunter-gatherers, the deepest parts of ourselves are still wild.

B And the whitethroat tells us that we don't have the monopoly on this feeling – it is something that other living creatures understand just as well. A liking for danger is part of our inheritance as mammals, as animals

C Because every now and then in springtime he will leave that little leafy home of his and launch himself skywards – so moved by his own eloquence that he must take to the wing and fly up, singing all the time, before gliding gently back down to safety.

D You must make your own mind up on these issues – but one thing you can't avoid is that this deliberate annual courting of danger is part of the way the whitethroat lives his life.

E Of course, it's not the same for everybody, not to the same extent. Most of us enjoy different levels and different forms of risk at different times, just like the whitethroat in his hedge. And it is all the better for the time afterwards, when we have risked and survived and returned safe and sound.

F The glories of the whitethroat's song demand this exhibition: the better and bolder and louder the song flight, the more likely the male is to attract a nice mate and keep that patch of prickly territory for himself. That's the evolutionary reason for it, anyway.

G You might take this opposite view because what the whitethroat shows us, amongst many other things, is why humans love tigers, love going on safari, love winter sports and fast cars, love riding horses and, above all, love all the vast, wild open spaces left on this planet. Most other creatures will give you the same message, too, if you study them. But the whitethroat does it in an especially vivid way.

Part 8

You are going to read an article in which four readers are suggesting good places to go wildlife watching. For questions **47 – 56**, choose from the sections (**A – D**). The sections may be chosen more than once.

In the exam, mark your answers **on a separate answer sheet.**

Which photographer

says there's a need to be flexible at a shoot?	47
admits to relying on instinctive decisions during a shoot?	48
consciously adopts a different type of behaviour during a shoot?	49
feels that aspects of a photographer's skill cannot be taught?	50
welcomes suggestions for shots from the subjects themselves?	51
is critical of recent developments on photography courses?	52
is keen to introduce new ideas in one branch of photography?	53
prefers not to take shots of people in a photographic studio?	54
tends to work to a set routine?	55
prefers not to do research about a subject before doing the shoot?	56

The critical moment

Four top photographers tell us how they get their extraordinary images.

A Oliver D'Amico

I loved photography from the moment I first picked up a camera and knew my life would be devoted to it. I don't think you can develop or learn a 'way of seeing' or a 'point of view'. It's something that's inside you. It's how you look at the world. I want my photographs not only to be real but to portray the essence of my subjects, too. To do that, you have to be patient – it can't be rushed. I prefer doing portraiture on location. On a subject's home ground you pick up certain hints that tell you personal things and they come up with ideas. During a session with an animal trainer who had a massive ego, he took the trunk of his beloved elephant Shyama and wrapped it around his neck like a necklace, and of course that was my picture. I'd never have thought of something that clever.

B Florian Ford

I don't know how my brain works, but I do know that I work really fast. My shoots don't vary: an hour to set up, an hour to take the shots. And the minute I walk into a room I know what I'm going to shoot, although what that is only becomes clear to me after seeing the result. So it's a subconscious process. You couldn't get those pictures in a million years if you took your time. I started taking pictures in the 1970s for all the beautiful reasons photography was known for. Then all of a sudden digital technology booms and darkrooms get annihilated from photography schools. But I really believe in the classical way. It all comes down to looking at a piece of art and dissecting it and understanding how it's put together. I think the most important thing is to go out in the world and see.

C Maggie Estevil

I think if you aren't fascinated by people, you'll never succeed as a portrait photographer, because your pictures will look cold. You don't have to know anything about the people in advance of the session, you just tap into them – it's a skill. Every shoot is different and you have to alter your approach accordingly. You have to try to get into people's heads, so that they can open up to you and give you something. Sometimes we chat first, but sometimes it's good for everyone to be fresh and tense when you start out. I use the technique of being cheeky and rude or asking my subjects to do ridiculous things, but I don't set out to upset anyone. I hope the viewer sees what I see. I think two words that would describe my work well are: humour and honesty.

D Petra Payne

I've always tried to push the boundaries of fashion photography. After all, why should a fashion photograph only talk about clothes? Why can't it talk about something else? I want my pictures to ask questions; I want people to think. You don't need to be technically great, because if you have a strong philosophy people will be moved by your pictures regardless. The most important thing is to figure out what you want to try and say. To make your name as a photographer, you have to have a unique point of view that the viewer can recognise as yours, otherwise you'll get lost in the mix. For me photography is about exploring – either myself or another place. The cynicism that exists in certain kinds of photography, and that pleasure of seeing oneself as a deep individualist that's not for me. We're a gregarious species made to live together. That's the point of view of my photography and the starting point of all my work.

Part 1

You **must** answer this question. Write your answer in **220 – 260** words in an appropriate style.

In the exam, you write your answer **on a separate answer sheet**.

---

1   Your class has listened to a radio discussion about whether increasing international tourism is always a good thing. You have made the notes below:

> **Pros and cons of international tourism**
> - enviromental impact
> - improved facilites
> - cultural understanding

> Some opinions expressed in the debate:
>
> "Travelling by plane isn't that bad and can't really affect climate change."
>
> "Facilities for tourists aren't always what locals want."
>
> "It's really important that different cultures understand each other."

Write an essay discussing two of the effects of international tourism in your notes. You should **explain which effect has been the most important**, **giving reasons** to support your opinion.

You may, if you wish, make use of the opinions expressed in the discussion, but you should use your own words as far as possible.

Part 2

Write an answer to one of the questions **2 – 4** in this part. Write your answer in **220 – 260** words in an appropriate style. In the exam, you write your answer **on a separate answer sheet**, and put the question number in the box at the top of the page.

---

2   Every year your college holds an end of year activity for all the students, and has asked everyone to send in proposals for this year's event.

You decide to write a proposal explaining any problems with last year's activity, suggesting activities for this year, and giving reasons to support your recommendations.

Write your **proposal**.

3   You see this advertisement on a television channel's website:

> ### Did you see our nature documentary series?
>
> We are considering making a second series of the nature documentary *Our wonderful planet*, and we'd like to hear viewers' opinions.
>
> Write us a review explaining what you liked or didn't like about the series, and clarifying whether you would like to see a second series.

Write your **review**.

4   You have returned from an adventure holiday with which there were several problems. The company has asked you to send in a report on the situation, explaining the problems and making recommendations for future holidays.

Write your **report**.

Part 1

You will hear three different extracts. For questions **1 – 6**, choose the answer (**A, B** or **C**) which fits best according to what you hear. There are two questions for each extract.

In the exam, you write your answers on **a separate answer sheet**.

Extract One

You hear part of a radio programme in which an expert art historian is talking about a picture.

1 He's chosen to talk about this particular picture because

    A   today would have been the artist's birthday.
    B   it illustrates certain aspects of the artist's technique.
    C   this is a significant time of year for the birds depicted.

2 What does he suggest about the artist?

    A   He wasn't always honest with people.
    B   He made a good deal of money from his work.
    C   He wasn't actually greatly interested in wildlife.

Extract Two

You hear part of a discussion about home improvements.

3 What does the woman suggest about most people who redesign their homes?

    A   They spend money on the wrong things.
    B   It's hard for them to visualise the end result.
    C   The plans they make are rather over-ambitious.

4 What is the man doing in his reply?

    A   disagreeing with her analysis of the situation
    B   suggesting a way of overcoming the problem she outlines
    C   reassuring her of the effectiveness of the software most people use

Extract Three

You hear part of a discussion about how wildlife films shown on TV are reviewed by journalists.

5   What do the two speakers agree about?

    A   Some animals don't make good subjects for these programmes.
    B   People now expect these programmes to be of a very high quality.
    C   Reviewers may be over-critical of certain aspects of these programmes.

6   The woman's fear is that reviewers of wildlife films are

    A   not focusing on the most important aspects of the films.
    B   being inconsistent in the way they review the films.
    C   not applying the same criteria to all the films.

Part 2

You will hear part of a presentation given by a psychologist called Simon Strang on the subject of boredom. For questions **7 – 14**, complete the sentences with a word or short phrase.

In the exam, mark your answers **on a separate answer sheet**.

Boredom

Simon says that a trip to Mars would take approximately

(7) .... to complete.

In the Space Agency simulation Simon mentions, both

(8) .... and individual behaviour will be studied.

Simon thinks that unhappy astronauts are likely to focus on the boring nature of their

(9) .... and other non-work issues.

Simon gives the example of an uninteresting **(10)** ....

as something which causes temporary boredom.

Simon uses the term **(11)** ....

boredom for feelings associated with routine jobs.

Dr Svendsen's definition of boredom sees it as an absence of

(12) ....

Simon says that it is wrong to regard **(13)** ....

as the opposite of boredom.

Simon suggests that a **(14)** ....

would be a good activity for bored children.

Part 3

You'll hear an interview with a woman called Emma Stoneham who works as a manager in the horse-racing industry. For questions **15 – 20**, choose the answer (**A**, **B**, **C** or **D**) which fits best according to what you hear.

In the exam, write your answers **on a separate answer sheet**.

---

15 Emma first got interested in horse racing as a result of

    A   a family connection.
    B   an educational visit.
    C   a passion for horses.
    D   peer-group pressure.

16 What does Emma say about her qualifications?

    A   She chose to study certain subjects against her father's wishes.
    B   She decided to do courses that dealt directly with horse racing.
    C   She did a postgraduate course that few people knew about.
    D   She was fortunate to be accepted on a specialist course.

17 How does Emma feel about what she calls the 'big names' in horse racing?

    A   She resents having to plan her events to suit them.
    B   She respects the contribution they make to the sport.
    C   She believes that they shouldn't receive special treatment.
    D   She accepts that she needs to put on particular events to attract them.

18 What does Emma particularly enjoy about race days?

    A   the range of people she meets
    B   the enthusiasm of her colleagues
    C   the challenge of dealing with the unexpected
    D   the pleasure of seeing people enjoying themselves

19 How did Emma feel after cancelling the midwinter race meeting?

    A   worried that inadequate precautions had been taken
    B   angry that bad weather hadn't been predicted
    C   satisfied that she'd made the right decision
    D   grateful for the good advice she'd received

20 As a result of cancelling the meeting, Emma has had to

    A   put on additional race meetings.
    B   make changes to her financial planning.
    C   sell some land belonging to the racecourse.
    D   postpone making improvements to facilities.

Part 4

You'll hear five creative people talking about receiving an award in recognition of their work.

In the exam, mark your answers **on a separate answer sheet**.

TASK ONE

For questions **21 – 25**, choose from the list (**A – H**) the creative activity each person is involved in.

TASK TWO

For questions **26 – 30**, choose from the list (**A – H**) how each person felt when they heard about winning the award.

While you listen you must complete both tasks.

A	novel writing
B	website design
C	television scriptwriting
D	landscape gardening
E	fashion design
F	documentary film-making
G	computer-game design
H	journalism

A	grateful for the publicity
B	surprised by the quality of the competition
C	sorry for the runners-up
D	embarrassed by all the attention
E	pleased to have proved someone wrong
F	disappointed by the ceremony itself
G	irritated by the judges
H	amused by other people's reactions

Speaker 1 21
Speaker 2 22
Speaker 3 23
Speaker 4 24
Speaker 5 25

Speaker 1 26
Speaker 2 27
Speaker 3 28
Speaker 4 29
Speaker 5 30

Part 1 (2 minutes)

The examiner will ask you one or two questions about yourself and what you think about everyday topics such as work or study, travel, holidays, daily life and routines.

- How do you usually travel round local places where you live? (Why?)
- What do you enjoy doing when you're with your family? (Why?)
- Where's a good place for tourists to visit in summer in your country? (Why?)

Part 2 (4 minutes)

Turn to the pictures on page 176, which **show people taking photographs**.

TAKING A PHOTOGRAPH

Candidate A, I'd like you to compare **two** of the pictures, and say **why the people might be taking the photographs and how important the photographs might be to them**.

Candidate B, **who do you think might keep their photographs the longest? (Why?)**

DOING SPORT

Turn to the pictures on page 178, which show people doing sport.

Candidate B, compare **two** of the pictures and say **why the people might have chosen to do these sports and how important it might be to do them regularly**.

Candidate A, **who do you think might value their sport the most? (Why?)**

Part 3 (4 minutes)

Turn to the task on page 177, which shows things many **people choose to spend their money on nowadays**.

Now, talk to each other about **why people choose to spend their money on these things**.

Now decide which one is **least important for people to spend a lot of money on**.

Part 4 (5 minutes)

Answer these questions.

- Do you think we spend too much money on material things? (Why / Why not?)
- In your opinion, should advertising be regulated more strictly? (Why / Why not?)
- Shopping has become a leisure activity for many people. Is this a good thing? (Why / Why not?)
- Do you think it's true that some people, like footballers or film actors, are paid far more money than they're really worth? (Why / Why not?)
- Some people say that we've lost sight of what's really important in life. What do you think? (Why?)
- Do you think it's really possible to be happy without spending any money? (Why / Why not?)

TEST 4

Part 1

For questions **1 – 8**, read the text below and decide which answer (**A**, **B**, **C** or **D**) best fits each gap. There is an example at the beginning (**0**).

In the exam, you mark your answers **on a separate answer sheet**.

Example:

| 0 | **A** set | **B** planned | **C** worked | **D** put |

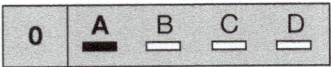

Football as an art form

When two filmmakers **(0)** .... out to make an art-house movie about the legendary French footballer Zinedine Zidane, they chose to film just one match. But **(1)** .... of following the progress of the game, the 90-minute film showed something that hadn't been seen before; the precise detailed movements of one player. Every **(2)** .... gesture is captured so that the audience can appreciate the player's grace, athleticism and competitiveness in **(3)** .... detail.

Those who aren't regular watchers of football will be astonished at how **(4)** .... Zidane becomes actively **(5)** .... in the game. For much of the time he moves around the field relatively slowly; saying nothing, expressing even less, and only occasionally **(6)** .... into a lethargic jog.

But when the ball arrives at his feet, there's a flurry of bewildering activity. The cameras struggle to **(7)** .... up, and the defenders don't stand a chance. In a few touches, a couple of checks and feints, Zidane has **(8)** .... them all behind. He crosses from the tightest of angles and his teammate has the simplest of shots to score a goal.

1	**A** alternative	**B** instead	**C** rather	**D** preference
2	**A** one	**B** single	**C** lone	**D** sole
3	**A** giant	**B** big	**C** vast	**D** great
4	**A** partly	**B** scarcely	**C** rarely	**D** hardly
5	**A** concerned	**B** involved	**C** associated	**D** regarded
6	**A** breaking	**B** changing	**C** opening	**D** starting
7	**A** take	**B** speed	**C** keep	**D** make
8	**A** missed	**B** left	**C** lost	**D** dropped

Part 2

For questions **9 – 16**, read the text below and think of the word which best fits each gap. Use only **one** word in each gap. There is an example at the beginning (**0**).

In the exam, you write your answers **IN CAPITAL LETTERS** on a separate answer sheet.

Example: | 0 | F | R | O | M | | | | | | | | | | | | |

An intriguing letter

Some years ago, I received a letter **(0)** ……… a stranger called Joanna King, asking for my advice. Joanna had an aunt **(9)** ……… had kept a diary from the age of 13 until she was 94. **(10)** ……… Joanna had never read these diaries, her aunt was known to be a woman **(11)** ……… strong opinions, and so she thought they might be interesting.

Joanna had read a memoir I'd written about my own grandmother, an ordinary woman with **(12)** ……… particular claim to fame, and it had made her wonder **(13)** ……… there was some value in her aunt's diaries as a social document. Could I suggest **(14)** ……… might be done with them?

I replied saying that the idea of someone keeping a diary over **(15)** ……… a long period was intriguing and that I'd love to read them myself. This was clearly the response Joanna had been hoping for because she then proceeded to offer them to me **(16)** ……… a source of inspiration for my own writing. I hadn't, in fact, meant that, but once suggested, the idea began to take hold in my mind.

Part 3

For questions **17 – 24**, read the text below. Use the word given in capitals at the end of some of the lines to form a word that fits in the gap **in the same line**. There is an example at the beginning (**0**).

In the exam, you write your answers **IN CAPITAL LETTERS** on a separate answer sheet.

Example: | 0 | E | N | T | I | T | L | E | D | | | | | | |

Time management

Julie Morganstern's book (**0**) ……….. *Time Management from the Inside Out* aims to help people organise their time better. **TITLE**

For Julie, getting yourself organised is what she calls a 'learnable' skill. One common reason she (**17**) ……….. for people not getting things done, **IDENTITY** be it tasks at work, study (**18**) ……….. , or things they hope to achieve in **OBJECT** their free time, is that they don't set aside a (**19**) ……….. time in which to **SPECIFY** do things.

In other words, they're always trying to fit new activities into an existing full schedule and (**20**) ……….. how long tasks are actually going to take. As a **ESTIMATE** result, they get behind schedule, and miss deadlines.

To avoid this, Julie suggests making a list of 'must do' tasks and putting a time (**21**) ……….. next to each. This means that a direct comparison can **ALLOW** be made between time spent on each task and how long you (**22**) ……….. **ORIGIN** thought it would take you. In no time at all, you'll be able to make an expert (**23**) ……….. about how long activities really take, meaning that you're more **JUDGE** (**24**) ……….. about how much you set out to achieve in the first place. **REAL**

Part 4

For questions **25 – 30**, complete the second sentence so that it has a similar meaning to the first sentence, using the word given. **Do not change the word given.** You must use between **three** and **six** words, including the word given. Here is an example (**0**).

Example:

0 Trevor persuaded his sister to enter the competition.

TALKED

Trevor .... entering the competition.

The gap can be filled with the words 'talked his sister into', so you write:

Example: | 0 | *TALKED HIS SISTER INTO*

In the exam, you write **only** the missing words **IN CAPITAL LETTERS on a separate answer sheet**.

---

25 The first employee to arrive in the morning should turn on the heating.

WHICHEVER

The heating should .... of staff arrives first in the morning.

26 We will have no choice but to reinforce the fence if those dogs keep getting through.

ALTERNATIVE

Reinforcing the fence .... if those dogs keep getting through.

27 Leila's interference in her sister's wedding plans has only caused trouble.

NOTHING

Leila's interference in her sister's wedding plans has led .... trouble.

28 The students did not return from the end-of-term party until dawn.

BEFORE

It was .... back from the end-of-term party.

29 "If you stay a bit longer, you'll enjoy yourself even more," said our host at the party.

MORE

Our host at the party said that the .... would enjoy ourselves.

30 We were horrified to see smoke coming out of the bedroom windows.

COULD

Much .... smoke coming out of the bedroom windows.

Part 5

You are going to read an extract from a book. For questions **31 – 36**, choose the answer (**A, B, C** or **D**) which you think fits best according to the text.

In the exam, you mark your answers **on a separate answer sheet**.

It's a commonplace of parenting and modern genetics that parents have little or no influence on the characters of their children. As a parent, you never know who you are going to get. Opportunities, health, prospects, accent, table manners – these might lie within your power to shape. But what really determines the sort of person who's coming to live with you is chance. Cheerful or neurotic, kind or greedy, curious or dull, expansive or shy and anywhere in between; it can be quite an affront to parental self-regard, just how much of the work has already been done. On the other hand, it can let you off the hook. The point is made for you as soon as you have more than one child; when two entirely different people emerge from their roughly similar chances in life.

Here in the cavernous basement kitchen at 3.55 a.m., in a single pool of light, as though on stage, is Theo Perowne, 18 years old, his formal education already long behind him, reclining on a tiled-back kitchen chair, his legs in tight black jeans, his feet in boots of soft black leather (paid for with his own money) crossed on the edge of the table. As unlike his sister Daisy as randomness will allow. He's drinking from a large tumbler of water. In the other hand he holds the folded-back music magazine he's reading. A studded leather jacket lies in a heap on the floor. Propped against a cupboard is his guitar in its case. It's already acquired a few steamer trunk labels – Trieste, Oakland, Hamburg, Val d'Isere. There's space for more. From a compact stereo player on a shelf above a library of cookery books comes the sound, like soft drizzle, of an all-night pop station.

Henry Perowne sometimes wonders if, in his youth, he could ever have guessed that he would one day father a blues musician. He himself was simply processed, without question or complaint, in a polished continuum from school, through medical school, to the dogged acquisition of clinical experience, in London, Southend-on-Sea, Newcastle, Bellevue Emergency Department in New York and London again. How have he and Rosalind, such dutiful, conventional types, given rise to such a free spirit? One who dresses, with a certain irony, in the style of the bohemian fifties, who won't read books or let himself be persuaded to stay on at school, who's rarely out of bed before lunchtime, whose passion is for mastery in all the nuances of the blues guitar tradition, Delta, Chicago, Mississippi, and for the success of his band, New Blue Rider. In the confined, gossipy world of British blues, Theo is spoken of as a man of promise, already mature in his grasp of the idiom, who might even one day walk with the gods, the British gods that is – Alexis Korner, John Mayall, Eric Clapton. Someone has written somewhere that Theo Perowne plays like an angel.

Naturally, his father agrees, despite his doubts about the limits of the form. He likes the blues well enough – in fact, he was the one who showed the nine-year-old Theo how it worked. After that, grandfather took over. But is there a lifetime's satisfaction in 12 bars of three obvious chords? Perhaps it's one of those cases of a microcosm giving you the whole world. Like a Spode dinner plate. Or a single cell. Or a Jane Austen novel. When player and listener together know the route so well, the pleasure is in the deviation, the unexpected turn against the grain.

And there's something in the loping authority of Theo's playing that revives for Henry the inexplicable lure of that simple progression. Theo is the sort of guitarist who plays in an open-eyed trance, without moving his body or ever glancing down at his hands. He concedes only an occasional thoughtful nod. Now and then, during a set he might tilt back his head to indicate to the others that he is 'going round' again. He carries himself on stage as he does in conversation, quietly, formally, protecting his privacy within a shell of friendly politeness. If he happens to spot his parents at the back of a crowd, he'll lift his left hand from the fret in a shy and private salute.

31 In the first paragraph, the writer suggests that parents

- **A** are often disappointed by their children's behaviour.
- **B** have relatively little impact on their children's personality.
- **C** sometimes leave too many aspects of child development to chance.
- **D** often make the mistake of trying to change their children's character.

32 Which phrase is used to suggest that parents are not to blame for how their children turn out?

- **A** anywhere in between (line **4**)
- **B** an affront to parental self-regard (line **5**)
- **C** let you off the hook (line **6**)
- **D** roughly similar chances (line **7**)

33 What do we learn about Theo Perowne in the second paragraph?

- **A** He has successfully completed his studies.
- **B** He is not particularly interested in travel.
- **C** He is not making a living as a musician.
- **D** He has little in common with his sister.

34 Theo's parents are described as the sort of people who

- **A** have let their careers take precedence over family
- **B** have found it quite difficult to settle down in life.
- **C** regret the rather predictable nature of their lives.
- **D** have always done what was expected of them.

35 With regard to his music, we learn that Theo is

- **A** dedicated to one particular style.
- **B** planning to form a band of his own.
- **C** unable to take it completely seriously.
- **D** already admired by some famous people.

36 According to the writer, how is blues music similar to a Jane Austen novel?

- **A** It has stood the test of time well.
- **B** It has an easily recognised structure.
- **C** It is open to individual interpretation.
- **D** It is full of unexpected changes of direction.

Part 6

You are going to read four commentaries on an exhibition at a museum. For questions **37 – 40**, choose from the extracts **A – D**. The extracts may be chosen more than once.

In the exam, you mark your answers **on a separate answer sheet**.

Commentator A

The current exhibition at the Bridgefoot Museum – Domestic Life in Renaissance Italy – is predictably pulling in the crowds, and there are fascinating treasures on display, even if some of the best are concealed in rather dimly lit corners. The 'Domestic Life' in the title rather suggests that you're going to see everything from the most fabulous riches to the kitchen sink. Sadly, this isn't the case, however. No doubt the truth is that what survives down the centuries, and what finds its way into museum collections, tends to be those objects of greatest value, at the time, given the quality of the materials used and the craftsmanship expended on them. There is a beautiful set of silver knives in the first room, which makes this point most powerfully. This, like other exhibits, is accompanied by a comprehensive caption board which provides background detail on its provenance and construction.

Commentator B

The Bridgefoot's latest blockbuster show transports us to home life in Italy in the 15th century. As we've come to except from such an experienced team, the exhibition is carefully laid out with clever use of space and imaginative lighting. This ensures that visitors move fluidly and comfortably between different aspects of daily existence. It's rather like intruding on a series of calm and unhurried domestic scenes from several centuries ago. Interpretation of the exhibits is supported by the somewhat uninspiring information panels, which unintentionally serve to underline just how unusual it would be to have all these items under the roof of a single home. One slight oversight perhaps is the lack of any truly commonplace objects, especially in the service areas. A few glimpses of the reality of life for the huge army of servants needed to support the lifestyle implied by the vast array of precious objects would have been welcome.

Commentator C

Any major exhibition with the words 'Italy' and 'Renaissance' in its title is bound to attract widespread interest and the long ,but briskly moving queue when I visited the Bridgefoot Museum last week was testimony to that. So it was with some relief that I discovered an imaginatively designed and spacious area which seemed to swallow up the visitor numbers with ease. I was able to quietly appreciate the glorious range of items on display; everything from an engraved early form of toothbrush to a scintillating set of gold tableware was competently shown off to its best by clever use of concealed lighting. Nearly all the items here are functional as well as being of great beauty and rather more detail on how they were used on a daily basis would have been welcome, rather than the somewhat dry descriptions listing the maker and materials used.

Commentator D

It's generally a treat to visit a special exhibition at the Bridgefoot Museum and the current offering should tick all the boxes for those of us who are fans of the Italian high renaissance. Popularity comes at a price, of course, and finding quite so many enthusiastic and vocal visitors in such close proximity to each other was something of a distraction from the interesting variety of precious objects on display. These are all loosely linked to Italian home life five centuries ago, but are joined by surprisingly uninformative captions positioned adjacent to the display cases. The treasures are imaginatively organised, however, following a range of themes: entertaining visitors, food preparation, personal hygiene, etc., but the generally subtle uplighting does favour the more substantial pieces at the expense of smaller, but no less fascinating, objects which make less impact than they deserve.

Which commentator

shares A's view about the range of exhibits on show?   37

has a different opinion to C regarding the written information available about the exhibits?   38

expresses a different view from the others about the impact of the number of people attending the exhibition?   39

shares D's views about the use of lighting at the exhibition?   40

Part 7

You are going to read an extract from an account of a sailing race. Six paragraphs have been removed from the article. Choose from the paragraphs **A – G** the one which fits each gap (**41 – 46**). There is one extra paragraph which you do not need to use.

In the exam, you mark your answers **on a separate answer sheet**.

Stiff breeze, no cocktails

Victor Mallet set sail on the yacht Moonblue 2 in a three-day race across the South China Sea which turned out to be packed with incident and excitement.

The sailing in the San Fernando Race was glorious; one of the best in the 30-year history of the event. From the outset, all the front-runners were spared the windless calms that can cause such frustration in events like this.

| 41 |

Apart from the unaccustomed speed, a few other things about *Moonblue 2* took some getting used to for me. There was the novelty of being on such a luxurious cruiser-racer, and the overall excellence of the food and drink on board. I wasn't used to such luxury, and I can't recall racing in a boat where you can take a shower when your period of watch comes to an end.

| 42 |

Despite such minor inconveniences, the race had been going well, but suddenly we hit a problem. Peter, the normally cheery skipper and owner of *Moonblue 2*, was shouting almost angrily from somewhere below, demanding to know where the cocktail blender was.

| 43 |

Peter repeated his question in frustration, adding: "Didn't anyone bring it back from the party at the yacht club?" We looked studiously into the darkness while we struggled to trim the sails and bring the boat under control. No, no one had brought it back from the pre-race party two nights earlier.

| 44 |

Once the penny had dropped, we realised it wasn't such a crazy request after all. It seemed that not for the first time, the high-strength line connecting the wheel to the rudder had snapped. Peter wanted the blender's long electric cable because it could be used to replace it. Just two hours later, three crew members – there were 13 of us on board altogether – fixed the steering not with the blender cable but with the help of a spare length of aerial cable, and we were able to continue racing. Part of the challenge of sailing for me is that anything can go wrong, even on a superbly equipped yacht such as *Moonblue 2*.

| 45 |

Such complicated yachts as *Moonblue 2* also require constant attention and minor adjustments to the steering, in contrast to an old-fashioned yacht that almost steers itself. For the crew on this trip, however, there were mercifully few sail changes during the race until the very end. But even at that stage, we still had one last small mishap to contend with. When we crossed the finishing line off San Fernando at midnight, two-and-a-half days after the start, a local captain who was supposed to guide us in to a safe anchorage took us straight on to a mudbank.

| 46 |

And of the 18 starters, *Moonblue 2* was second to finish, a fantastic result overall – with or without the cocktail blender!

A This had become apparent the previous weekend on a pre-race practice run when first the propeller had been entangled in rope and then again in industrial plastic in the space of an hour. On each occasion one of the crew had had to dive into the water with a knife and a pair of goggles to clear the debris.

B But any large boat, however stylish, also has its drawbacks. In rough seas it was tricky getting from one end of the spacious cabin to the other because the hand holds were so far apart.

C After all, the pre-race discussion had revolved largely around the issue of how just such a situation might be dealt with. Fortunately, however, an unexpected solution was at hand.

D It could have been worse, however. Our Australian rival, *Strewth*, was led into a reef with a crunch, so we actually had quite a lucky escape.

E To those of us out on deck, however, this didn't seem to be quite the moment for any kind of a drink. It was eight hours into the race, there was a stiff breeze, rough waves and the steering had just failed completely.

F This wasn't an entirely enjoyable time for me, though, as in the initial 36 hours we were driven by a north-east monsoon wind that sometimes whipped up a rough and uncomfortable sea. On the plus side, however, we sped southwards under full sail, making amazing time.

G A few uncomfortable moments passed, nobody wanting to break this piece of news to him. Then we we suddenly saw what he was on about.

Part 8

You are going to read an article about novels set in places that the author isn't actually familiar with. For questions **47 – 56**, choose from the novels (**A – D**). The novels may be chosen more than once.

In the exam, mark your answers **on a separate answer sheet.**

About which novel is the following stated?

It attracted a criticism which pleased its author.	47
It contrasts the lives of people living in different locations.	48
It was the author's first book of this type.	49
It fails to make all of its local references clear to the reader.	50
It's regarded as one of the best novels of its type.	51
It may give a rather unrealistic impression of the country concerned.	52
It contains at least one inaccurate detail.	53
It was written by somebody who chose to visit the area only briefly.	54
It was praised for the way it describes ordinary people.	55
Its writer lacked the financial resources to visit the area.	56

Gullible's travels

Novels are works of the imagination. But what happens when an author writes about a part of the world they've never been to?

A Something like a house
A few years ago, presenter Mark Lawson conducted a memorable radio interview with the author Sid Smith who had just won an award for his debut novel. Set in China during the Cultural Revolution, the novel received critical acclaim for its evocation of peasant life. Lawson, impressed by Smith's depiction, asked if he spoke fluent Chinese. Smith said no, he didn't. Lawson asked if he'd worked in China. No, he hadn't. At this point Lawson became agitated. "But you've *been* to China," he said. There was a short pause, followed by Smith's calm assertion that actually he hadn't. Lawson was right to be astounded. Although set in the past and told through an Englishman, the story is full of odd details about life in the China of the period that you'd think would take years of first-hand experience to note. Not just physical things, such as the river sand in the bottom of a cup of tea, but social niceties such as Madame Tao judging her neighbours by how far up the valley they collect their water. What was most enjoyable about the interview, though, was Smith's refusal to be even slightly apologetic. He found his China in the London Library, from films, newspapers and the internet. Who's to say that this gave him any less valid a picture of China than one he might have gained on a trip to modern-day Beijing?

B Waterland
A novel often cited as exemplary in depicting place is *Waterland,* Graham Swift's saga of several generations of Fenlanders. The Crick family lacks ambition and drive, driven to 'unquiet and sleep-defeating thoughts' by the insistently flat, monotonous land; while the Atkinsons, who live on the only hill, get 'ideas', spot gaps in the market, and make a fortune brewing beer. As an example of how landscapes shape characters it is perhaps unmatched in contemporary fiction. Yet, Swift is not a Fenlander, and according to his agent made just a few fleeting visits to the Fens after he'd begun his novel. Swift lives in London and presumably could have travelled to the Fens more often had he wished to. Is it possible that a partial knowledge of the place suited him?

C Welcome to hard times
American novelist E. L. Doctorow wrote this western 'never having been west of Ohio.' Although it's a wholly satisfying example of the genre, such an approach is vulnerable to errors. After the book came out, an old lady from Texas wrote to Doctorow to say that she could tell he'd never been out west because of the character who 'made himself a dinner of the roasted haunch of a prairie dog'; a prairie dog's haunch, she said, 'wouldn't fill a teaspoon'. Doctorow was delighted and let the line stand in future editions, being 'leery of perfection'. Too much accuracy, he realised, might suck the life out of the novel.

D Eclipse of the sun
Too ardent a straining for accuracy is a charge that could be levelled at Phil Whitaker's novel, *Eclipse of the sun*. Set in a fictional town in an imagined India (Whitaker has said that he couldn't afford the trip), the novel has clearly been meticulously researched. He has grasped the implied insult of answering in English a question posed in Marathi; that Indians love the word 'auspicious'. He gives us *bidis* and *rikkas*, *crores* and *lakhs*, plates of *jalebi* and the performances of *yagnas* while resisting the urge to explain. The BBC's India correspondent Mark Tully found no fault in its depiction of small-town India. Yet Whitaker runs the risk of making his characters too Indian, too perfect. Perhaps if he'd been to India he'd have found a people that were odder, less typical, than the country he discovered through research. Or perhaps, if he'd gone to India, he wouldn't have written the book at all – he might have become aware of how much he didn't know.

Part 1

You must answer this question. Write your answer in **220 – 260** words in an appropriate style.

In the exam, you write your answer **on a separate answer sheet**.

---

1   Your class has attended a panel discussion on ways individuals can really make a difference to some of the important environmental issues in today's world. You have made the notes below:

> **Ways individuals can make a difference to environmental issues**
> - avoid plastic
> - raise awareness
> - choose how to travel

> Some opinions expressed in the discussion:
>
> "No-one cares about plastic – it's so easy to use and it's everywhere."
>
> "Putting leaflets through people's doors can help environmental campaigns if the people bother to read them."
>
> "It's impossible to change the way we travel – it's part of everyday life."

Write an essay discussing two of the ways in your notes in which individuals might make a difference to environmental issues. You should **explain which way you think is more effective, giving reasons** to support your opinion.

You may, if you wish, make use of the opinions expressed in the debate, but you should use your own words as far as possible.

Part 2

Write an answer to **one** of the questions **2 – 4** in this part. Write your answer in **220 – 260** words in an appropriate style. In the exam, you write your answer **on a separate answer sheet**, and put the question number in the box at the top of the page.

---

2   You have recently been on a two-day training course to improve your time-management skills. Your line manager has asked you to write a short report on the course, describing what the course was like, how useful it was and whether you would recommend it to colleagues.

   Write your **report**.

3   Your college wants to spend some money improving facilities for students learning foreign languages, and has asked for proposals. Write a proposal explaining why the current facilities need improvement, and making recommendations for how the money should be spent.

   Write your **proposal**.

4   You have received this email from an English-speaking friend:

   > Hi!
   >
   > How are you?
   >
   > I've got to do some research into young people and their lifestyles, and it'd be great if you could tell me something about young people's lives in your town. Do they leave home to go to university? How about the job situation? Do they take part-time jobs while they're studying?
   >
   > Thanks for your help, and I hope we can meet up soon.
   >
   > All the best,
   >
   > Jo

   Write your **email**.

Part 1

You will hear three different extracts. For questions **1 – 6**, choose the answer (**A, B or C**) which fits best according to what you hear. There are two questions for each extract.

In the exam, you write your answers **on a separate answer sheet**.

Extract One

You hear part of an interview with the editor of a book about pop music.

1   He says members of the public often wrongly assumes that

    A   large numbers of people work on the book.
    B   their queries can be answered very quickly.
    C   the book is actually compiled by non-experts.

2   How does he feel about most of the complaints he receives?

    A   He's irritated when they focus on unimportant details.
    B   He's pleased that people take the book so seriously.
    C   He's not particularly interested in them.

Extract Two

You hear part of a radio programme about a photographic competition.

3   What is the presenter doing?

    A   Announcing a new theme for the competition.
    B   Encouraging listeners to enter the competition.
    C   Explaining how the competition is being judged.

4   What do we learn about last week's winner?

    A   He selected the location of the shot in advance.
    B   He got his subjects to pose for the shot.
    C   He only got one shot of this subject.

Extract Three

You hear part of a discussion about playing games.

5   What does the man suggest about his family?

    A   Participation in group activities is optional.
    B   Time spent together is regarded as valuable.
    C   Children may choose how to spend their free time.

6   He says that when asked to give a performance, some of his relations feel

    A   reluctant to join in.
    B   amused at the idea.
    C   honoured to be asked.

Part 2

You will hear part of a presentation by a naturalist about a type of bird called a crane. For questions **7 – 14,** complete the sentences with a word or short phrase.

In the exam, you mark your answers **on a separate answer sheet.**

Cranes

In parts of Asia, the crane is thought to represent both

(7) .... and ....

The total population of the Blue Crane stands at around

(8) .... individuals.

The crane's usual habitat is in areas of **(9)** ....

which are getting scarcer in Africa.

Both small animals and **(10)** ....

are given as examples of what cranes eat.

Cranes often collide with the **(11)** ....

that are now found across southern Africa.

Crane conservation in South Africa is co-ordinated by an organisation called the

(12) ....

In one conservation scheme, local women both **(13)** .... and ....

like cranes when looking after young chicks.

The movement of cranes is also being tracked through the use of tiny

(14) .... linked to airports.

Part 3

You will hear an interview in which a circus owner called Tony Morland and his personal assistant, a woman called Anita Meadows, are talking about their work. For questions **15 – 20**, choose the answer (**A**, **B**, **C** or **D**) which fits best according to what you hear.

In the exam, write your answers **on a separate answer sheet**.

---

15 Why did Tony first go to work in a circus?

    A   It was a family tradition.
    B   It was his childhood ambition.
    C   He felt it was time to leave home.
    D   He wanted to avoid further education.

16 When he first joined a circus, Tony was

    A   disappointed not to work with animals.
    B   frustrated by his lack of experience.
    C   determined to develop his career.
    D   keen to develop his own act.

17 Tony recognises that he only managed to start his own circus because

    A   he was able to negotiate a loan.
    B   he joined forces with a colleague.
    C   he received a very generous gift.
    D   he employed a skilful secretary.

18 Initially, Anita regarded joining the circus as a way of

    A   indulging her love of travel.
    B   making her dream come true.
    C   improving her career prospects.
    D   putting her problems behind her.

19 At what point did Anita become Tony's personal assistant?

    A   as soon as the post fell vacant
    B   once she had gained further qualifications
    C   when he decided to give up doing office work
    D   over a period of time as her range of duties increased

20 What does Anita appreciate most about working with Tony?

    A   the high standards he sets
    B   his sensitivity to her needs
    C   his attitude towards the work
    D   the level of responsibility he gives her

TEST 4

LISTENING

Part 4

You will hear five short extracts in which people are talking about study holidays they have been on.

In the exam, mark your answers **on a separate answer sheet**.

TASK ONE

For questions **21 – 25**, choose from the list (**A – H**) what each person studied on their course.

While you listen you must complete both tasks.

- **A** a foreign language
- **B** cookery
- **C** creative writing
- **D** drama
- **E** music
- **F** painting
- **G** pottery
- **H** photography

Speaker 1 [21]
Speaker 2 [22]
Speaker 3 [23]
Speaker 4 [24]
Speaker 5 [25]

TASK TWO

For questions **26 – 30**, choose from the list (**A – H**) what each person says about their course.

- **A** I appreciated the flexibility of the staff.
- **B** I'd have liked a change of scene occasionally.
- **C** I enjoyed observing the other people.
- **D** I'd have liked more guidance from the tutor.
- **E** I was pleased to work on my own.
- **F** I was glad to be kept fully occupied.
- **G** I liked the great variety of people I met.
- **H** I'd have liked more time to practice.

Speaker 1 [26]
Speaker 2 [27]
Speaker 3 [28]
Speaker 4 [29]
Speaker 5 [30]

Part 1 (2 minutes)

The examiner will ask you one or two questions about yourself and what you think about everyday topics such as work or study, travel, holidays, daily life and routines.

- Do you spend more or less time watching television than when you were younger? (Why?)
- Do you share the interests of other members of your family? (Why / Why not?)
- Do you prefer having long holidays, or taking short breaks? (Why?)

Part 2 (4 minutes)

Turn to the pictures on page 179, which show **people working in different situations**.

PEOPLE WORKING

Candidate A, I'd like you to compare **two** of the pictures, and say **what the people might find hard about working in these situations, and how easy it might be to deal with any problems**.

Candidate B, **who do you think needs the greatest skill? (Why?)**

ADVENTURE ACTIVITIES

Turn to the pictures on page 180, which show **people taking part in adventure activities**.

Candidate B, compare **two** of the pictures and say **what you think people might enjoy about taking part in activities like these, and how difficult it might be to do them well**.

Candidate A, **which activity do you think would be most difficult for most people? (Why?)**

Part 3 (4 minutes)

Turn to the diagram on page 181, which shows **ways in which people try to solve problems for people who live in cities**.

Now, talk to each other about how **effective these ways of solving problems are for people who live in cities**.

Now decide **which solution would help the greatest number of people in a city**.

Part 4 (5 minutes)

Answer these questions.

- How important is it to plan new buildings in cities? (Why / Why not?)
- Should families in cities be allowed to own more than one car? (Why / Why not?)
- How important are tourists for the development of cities? (Why?)
- Do you think that science-fiction films give an accurate idea of cities of the future? (Why / Why not?)
- What do you think makes a city an ideal place to live in?
- Some people choose to move from the city to the country. Do you think life in the country is really better? (Why / why not?)

TEST 5

Part 1

For questions **1 – 8**, read the text below and decide which answer (**A**, **B**, **C** or **D**) best fits each gap. There is an example at the beginning (**0**).

In the exam, you mark your answers **on a separate answer sheet**.

Example:

0   A know   B think   C name   D tell

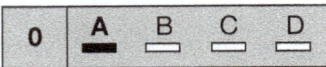

A shirt of two sports

It was the French tennis star René Lacoste who was responsible for popularising the polo shirt as we **(0)** .... it today. But he **(1)** .... his design on an existing garment, which was already being worn by polo teams in South America.

In the 1930s, polo had become an Olympic sport, and was popular in South America as well as in Europe. The company La Martina became the official supplier of polo kit and clothing to the Argentine national team, and helped to promote the polo shirt as a fashion **(2)** ....

In 1933, Lacoste joined **(3)** .... with André Gillier, then owner of France's largest knitwear company, to manufacture the shirt. It was smart enough to **(4)** .... with the dress regulations that tennis players had to follow, **(5)** .... remaining cool and flexible enough to provide an attractive **(6)** .... to the long-sleeved, starched-collar shirts that many players were still **(7)** .... to wear. Indeed, despite its name, it's now the world of tennis which the polo shirt is most commonly **(8)** .... with.

1	A depended	B founded	C sourced	D based
2	A issue	B matter	C object	D item
3	A aims	B forces	C teams	D links
4	A adhere	B conform	C comply	D abide
5	A albeit	B whilst	C whereas	D thereby
6	A alternative	B choice	C option	D preference
7	A obeying	B insisting	C accepting	D tending
8	A concerned	B regarded	C associated	D respected

Part 2

For questions **9 – 16**, read the text below and think of the word which best fits each gap. Use only **one** word in each gap. There is an example at the beginning (**0**).

In the exam, you write your answers **IN CAPITAL LETTERS on a separate answer sheet**.

Example: 0 W H E N

The blood moon

A lunar eclipse occurs (**0**) ……….. the Earth's shadow falls directly onto the moon. (**9**) ……….. happens as a result is that the moon stops being a silvery white colour and turns coppery red instead: the sort of colour usually only seen in the sky at dawn or sunset. An astronaut on the moon, looking towards the Earth (**10**) ……….. a lunar eclipse, would see a black disc, surrounded by a bright red ring. It's the light from this red ring (**11**) ……….. is reflected back to the dark Earth from the moon's surface. In ancient times, long (**12**) ……….. any of this was understood, the lunar eclipse was known (**13**) ……….. a blood moon and was thought to be an omen of disaster.

Total eclipses can only occur when there is a full moon, and then only if it is lined (**14**) ……….. with the Earth in a particular way. (**15**) ……….. easily obscured by cloud cover, blood moons are fairly common, and it's relatively easy to calculate where and when you might be (**16**) ……….. to see one.

Part 3

For questions **17 – 24**, read the text below. Use the word given in capitals at the end of some of the lines to form a word that fits in the gap **in the same line**. There is an example at the beginning (**0**).

In the exam, you write your answers **IN CAPITAL LETTERS** on a separate answer sheet.

Example: | 0 | F | I | N | D | I | N | G | S | | | | | | | | |

A real test of manhood

The (**0**) .... of a recent study indicate that women find men who are both willing and able to lend a hand with the housework more	**FIND**
(**17**) .... Although this will cause some raised eyebrows, to my	**ATTRACT**
mind it is a (**18**) .... of the blindingly obvious.	**STATE**
Take the example of my grandfather: a hospital (**19**) .... and competitive sailor, who was also a dab hand at needlework. As a child, I used to watch his enormous fingers flashing away at	**SURGERY**
an (**20**) .... intricate piece of sewing and think him the absolute	**ESPECIAL**
model of a manly man: someone who found a quiet (**21**) .... in	**SATISFY**
the patient (**22**) .... of practical tasks, to a high degree of perfection.	**EXECUTE**
For me, the real mystery is why so many men allow themselves to exist in a state of humiliating domestic (**23**) .... for so long. I think	**COMPETENT**
all men should be able to cook and iron. After all, isn't learning to fend for yourself outside the nest the first (**24**) .... test of manhood?	**ESSENCE**

Part 4

For questions **25 – 30**, complete the second sentence so that it has a similar meaning to the first sentence, using the word given. **Do not change the word given**. You must use between **three** and **six** words, including the word given. Here is an example (**0**).

Example:

0 Trevor persuaded his sister to enter the competition.

   TALKED

   Trevor .... entering the competition.

The gap can be filled with the words 'talked his sister into', so you write:

Example: | 0 | TALKED HIS SISTER INTO |

In the exam, you write **only** the missing words **IN CAPITAL LETTERS on a separate answer sheet.**

---

25 Repairing that old computer is pointless in my view.

   POINT

   I can .... that old computer being repaired.

26 "The company benefits from looking after its customers," said the chairperson.

   INTERESTS

   According to the chairperson, it is .... to look after its customers.

27 Jack went to the doctor who said he had chicken pox.

   SUFFERING

   Jack went to the doctor who .... chicken pox.

28 The ban on parking in the city centre is probably going to be very unpopular.

   LIKELY

   It .... ban in the city centre will be a very unpopular move.

29 The police acted quickly and prevented a fight between rival groups developing.

   PART

   Quick .... the police prevented a fight between rival groups developing.

30 We missed the train because we had arrived at the station late.

   BY

   The train .... we arrived at the station.

Part 5

You are going to read a businessman. For questions **31 – 36**, choose the answer (**A**, **B**, **C** or **D**) which you think fits best according to the text.

In the exam, you mark your answers **on a separate answer sheet.**

The codfather

The cod, the species of fish that features in the famous British dish 'fish and chips', could soon make the leap out of the frying pan and into popular culture according to Karol Rzepkowski, an effervescent Scot of Polish descent. "Someone approached us specifically with a view to making iPod covers out of cod skins – it's seen as an alternative to snake skin for the fashion industry," laughs 42-year-old Karol, managing director of Johnson Seafarms, an organic cod farm, located in the Shetland Isles. Lifestyle entrepreneurs may have to wait though, because the main target market for Karol's carefully reared cod is clearly a consumer armed with knife and fork rather than a music player.

Along with business partner Laurent Viguie, Karol has put enormous effort into the technology and diversification that they hope will bring sea farming up to date with a profitable, environmentally friendly, cod-farming venture. All of this is literally oceans away from the chance meeting that brought together two businessmen with the clout to push forward a scheme deemed outlandish by most people in the business.

Karol and Laurent struck up a friendship whilst on a diving trip off the Caribbean island of Grenada in 1999, and realised that their different business experience would make them into a formidable team. Laurent was a trained lawyer, restaurateur and high-profile figure in the music industry, while Karol was running Grenada's biggest leisure company, having grown up helping at his father's delicatessen in Edinburgh. Karel has never flinched from hard work. "One day, it might be nice to have a holiday..." he says wistfully.

Life in Grenada was good, but Karol was married to a Shetlander and wanted his 12-year-old son to grow up with a good education as well as personal freedom: "Somewhere he can walk out of the door at nine in the morning and we don't need to worry if he's not back until nine at night." Most people might think of moving to a sleepy village within commuting distance of a big city, but he found his idyll on a scattering of islands that are closer to the Arctic Circle than to London, where puffins outnumber people by ten to one.

After moving to Shetland, Karol found employment as marketing director at Johnson Seafarms, a small, family-owned company, which mostly reared salmon. Two fishing issues featured on the public agenda around that time: a spate of public-health scares over the chemicals used to farm salmon, and the plight of wild cod as over-fishing devastated shoals in the North Sea. Cod stocks there have plummeted 75 percent over the past 15 years, bringing the lynchpin of UK cuisine almost to the cusp of extinction – yet Britons tuck into some 170,000 tonnes of the fish every year.

The solution was obvious for Karol, "Farmed salmon was becoming a tainted industry in people's minds. I said: why don't we just move into another species?" but everyone was rather taken aback at the idea. After convincing sceptical colleagues, he faced the much tougher task of persuading hard-boiled financiers to **58** stump up millions of pounds for an unprecedented experiment. Karol enlisted the support of his old friend Laurent who, convinced that the plan had potential, decided to join forces with Karol and take **62** over the company. With money at Johnson Seafarms fast running out, the pair headed to London to seek emergency funds of £21m. "There was a great deal of **65** misgiving, but the people who were most reticent were the ones who ended up investing," adds Karol. With enough investors interested the company went through the process known as due diligence, which saw zealous **69** lawyers and accountants descending on the Shetland Isles to scour the paperwork and check every last detail. "It was a major cliff-hanger – at any moment it could have fallen flat on its face," says Karol. When it didn't, he says, the biggest thrill was being able to call the company's 27 employees and tell them their jobs were safe. The end of the funding drama was the start of real work: farming a new species of fish in a way that would address increasingly pressing environmental and ethical concerns.

31 How has Karol reacted to the idea of making cod-skin iPod covers?

　　A　It's not his main priority at the moment.
　　B　He thinks that it is a ridiculous suggestion.
　　C　He cannot see them catching on as a fashion item.
　　D　It is something he is looking forward to trying out.

32 Karol and his business partner, Laurent, met

　　A　whilst both were on holiday in Grenada.
　　B　because of a shared leisure interest.
　　C　as a result of their business dealings.
　　D　though a contact in the food industry.

33 Why did Karol move to Shetland?

　　A　He had the offer of a job in the area.
　　B　He had family responsibilities on the islands.
　　C　He could see there would be business opportunities there.
　　D　He wanted his family to benefit from a particular lifestyle.

34 What problem was *Johnson Seafarms* facing when Karol first worked there?

　　A　a decline in the local fishing industry
　　B　the limited resources available to the company
　　C　a loss of public confidence in fish-farming methods
　　D　poor health affecting the main type of fish it produced

35 How did Karol's colleagues react to his proposed solution to the company's problems?

　　A　They refused to cooperate with him.
　　B　They eventually accepted his suggestion.
　　C　They remained unconvinced that it would be successful.
　　D　They immediately realised it was their only hope of survival.

36 Which phrase from the sixth paragraph is used to emphasise how keen someone was to do something properly?

　　A　hard-boiled (line **58**)
　　B　join forces (line **62**)
　　C　a great deal of misgiving (line **65**)
　　D　zealous (line **69**)

Part 6

You are going to read four extracts in which journalists are commenting on a recent report on the subject of business travel. For questions **37 – 40**, choose from the journalists **A – D**. The journalists may be chosen more than once.

In the exam, you mark your answers **on a separate answer sheet.**

Journalist A
In the era of instant online communication and all that goes with it, you'd be forgiven for thinking that the days of business travel might be numbered. Yet, according to a well-researched report from *International Traveller Magazine*, it continues to go from strength to strength. Although viewed with deep suspicion by corporate finance departments, business travel is proving to be highly resilient, a trend borne out by sales of business-class airline seats. The report correctly puts this down to the fact that companies recognise the overwhelming need to grow and prosper by establishing strong bonds with both customers and suppliers. In the words of the report, they believe this to be most effectively achieved via face-to-face interaction, not least because the chances of cross-cultural misunderstanding seem to be greater when interaction only takes place online. So whether it's focused meetings between key individuals or a presence at trade shows and conferences, travel pays dividends in the long run.

Journalist B
Some commentators predict that advances in digital technology will eventually mean an end to business travel as we know it. Not so the authors of a report commissioned by *International Traveller Magazine*, who make a solid case for the ongoing need for business travel in the digital age. This will strike a chord with anyone who's tried to do business solely online, and found it to be no substitute for visiting or entertaining clients in person. The report quotes many instances of deals being struck thanks to just the kind of bonding that takes place over lunch, but which is so hard to achieve in a video link. It also describes other occasions when awkward video conferences led nowhere because neither side was sure whose cultural conventions to follow in cyber space. In any case, where is the data to show that business travel is on the wane? Not in the hospitality sector for sure, because that's booming.

Journalist C
Business travel continues to be seen as a necessity and occasionally a privilege by the corporate sector as a whole, and there are various reasons for that. But to read the report that appeared recently in *International Traveller Magazine*, you'd think the digital revolution had never happened. Its contention that only face-to-face meetings are good for business deals seems rather wide of the mark, when finance departments are known to be cutting business-travel budgets across the board. You wonder if the authors of the report have been talking to the right people? Similarly far-fetched is the idea quoted in the report that it's harder to do business across cultures online. Surely, it's by breaking down exactly those barriers that the internet has facilitated international trade? That there are benefits to having physical meetings with business partners and making new contacts at conferences is undeniable, but the internet is changing things.

Journalist D
How can you do international business without sometimes meeting your overseas colleagues and the people you trade with? An increasing understanding of cross-cultural differences has served to reinforce the argument for business travel and the closer interactions it brings. But this is rather overstated in an otherwise very balanced report in *International Traveller Magazine*. Anything you can achieve face-to-face can also be achieved online if approached in the right way. It seems, however, that business travel isn't in decline, and the report provides indisputable figures to back up this claim. The cynic in me is inclined to think that this has more to do with the status it confers on executives than with the business case for it, however. Advocates of stay-at-home substitutes for business travel may be more vocal than ever, but there's little sign of them having much impact.

Which journalist

shares journalist A's view regarding the reasons for the continued importance of business travel?   37

has a different view from the others regarding whether there is evidence for the continued popularity of business travel?   38

has a similar view to C regarding the likelihood of cross-cultural misunderstandings occurring online?   39

has a different view from B regarding the extent to which the findings of the report can generally be relied upon?   40

Part 7

You are going to read an article about a designer. Six paragraphs have been removed from the article. Choose from the paragraphs **A – G** the one which fits each gap (**41 – 46**). There is one extra paragraph which you do not need to use.

In the exam, you mark your answers **on a separate answer sheet**.

A biological approach to architecture

A spider's web is stronger than almost any material manufactured by man. Yet the spider produces it with nothing more than dead flies and a little water. It seems we still have a lot to learn. One person who makes his living by drawing inspiration from nature's handiwork is Michael Pawlyn, the founder of Exploration Architecture, which specialises in biomimicry. As someone who's devoted his career to studying shapes, materials and designs, he says it's foolish for any architect to ignore nature's 3.8 billion-year research-and-development programme.

41

"Nature's absolutely ruthless in rooting out all the failed mutations and variations. What we have left is an amazing catalogue of success stories," he explains in crisp, carefully constructed sentences. "We often think that humans are all-knowing and all-powerful, but there's still a huge amount we can glean." We're talking in his minimalist apartment in east London. "I love the idea of open-plan living," he says. As you'd expect from such a visual person, the apartment is studded with eye-catching furniture and some striking art.

42

It was only while working on the Eden Project that he realised he could recombine those adolescent passions. After David Kirkland, one of the project's chief architects, dreamt up the concept of building intersecting spheres, Pawlyn set about making it work. Most examples of spherical geometry in nature involved hexagons or pentagons. "So, we developed some geodesic grids inspired by the work of Buckminster Fuller. For the spheres, there was quite a complex resolution to achieve at the junctions, and for that we looked at dragonfly wings."

43

This belief in finding natural solutions to architectural challenges was reinforced when he attended a short course at Schumacher College in Devon run by leading environmentalists Amory Lovins, co-founder of the Rocky Mountain Institute, and Janine Benyus, author of one of the first books on biomimicry. "I learnt more in those few days than in years of going to conferences," he remembers.

44

Pawlyn acknowledges that it can be a struggle to fund such futuristic ideas. After all, in most cases architects can only be as creative as their clients, and their finances, allow. But he senses there's a growing appetite for more creative environmental solutions and longer payback periods. "I think we really do need to promote a longer inter-generational idea of timescales," he says.

45

These are seen as polar opposites and what we really need to do is to try and bring the management of the finances together with the knowledge of the natural world to develop solutions that are fit for the long term.

46

During his time there, Pawlyn has observed a process of urban evolution, common to many cities, which he likens to the natural world. Artists are the first people to move into semi-derelict areas, in search of cheap space and characterful buildings. The next wave of 'colonisers' are often the architects and designers, followed by media types and creatives. The process is very like ecological succession and is completed by the arrival of merchant bankers.

A After almost 20 years in the apartment, Pawlyn is decamping to north London, to gain access to more space. But he says he'll retain his attachment to what is now a fashionably cool district popular among start-up tech entrepreneurs.

B As a teenager, however, accompanying his oil executive father to various postings in mainland Europe and the Middle East, Pawlyn developed an interest in three areas: design, biology and the environment. But these interests diverged as he pursued a conventional architecture training at university.

C He points to the example of a 17th-century building which was able to repair its roof because the builders had planted a grove of oak trees at the same time, providing the wood for an eventual repair. He feels that there's still an unhelpful divide between economy and ecology at the moment.

D His work on creating the famous biomes at the Eden Project in southwest England, for example, was partly inspired by studying the structure of soap bubbles and dragonfly wings. More recently he's been looking at urchin spines, molluscs, water lilies and boxfish exoskeletons for fresh ideas.

E There are always human dimensions to consider in renovating urban buildings, be they cultural, historical or psychological. "Architecture is much more than just a technical discipline," he says.

F So strong was Pawlyn's conviction that he set up his own architectural practice inspired by their ideas. The aim is to produce "biologically inspired architecture to address some of the key environmental challenges of our age", such as climate change and mass urbanisation.

G Such was the simplicity and efficiency of the design that, remarkably, the entire structure weighed less than the air inside it. "It saved resources, it saved energy and it actually worked out a lot cheaper than a conventional glass structure would've been," he says.

Part 8

You are going to read an article about call-centre workers who give advice over the phone. For questions **47 – 56**, choose from the sections (**A – D**). The sections may be chosen more than once.

In the exam, you mark your answers **on a separate answer sheet**.

Which of the call-centre workers

advises people on the legal background to a problem?	47
enjoys the variety of things which people call about?	48
used to find it hard to work with only a spoken description of people's problems?	49
gets back to certain callers within a given period of time?	50
can arrange for an expert to visit callers at home?	51
has identified a regular pattern in calls on certain subjects?	52
finds some people have unrealistic expectations of the service provided?	53
sometimes has to correct information obtained elsewhere?	54
was initially apprehensive about the type of problems people would call with?	55
looks forward to the challenge of unexpected individual enquiries?	56

Give us a call

What's it like dealing with people on the phone all day?
We asked four call-centre workers

A Claire Lippold: Bat Conservation

I did a degree in biology, and studied bats as part of my thesis. When I saw the ad for this job I thought it would be perfect for me. We get about 10,000 calls a year, many from people worried that if they have bats in their loft they can't have any building work done. They need the right advice, because the law protects bats. We're contracted by an organisation called Natural England to arrange a service whereby anybody with bats on their property can have a specialist volunteer come out and give information and advice about the creatures they're living with. Generally, once they have the information, they're happy. It's the sign of a really green environment if you have bats. One of the most common myths we have to explode is that bats always turn left when they leave roofs. Apparently, that was printed in a magazine recently, so we got a clutch of calls about it. We also get people calling and humming the entire Batman theme tune down the phone. The jokes are pretty predictable, I'm afraid.

B Anthea McNufty: National Health Service

Although I'd worked in nursing for many years, I remember the dread of what the calls might be about on my first day. But they give you so much training before you're let loose that you can handle it. It was a bit difficult not having the physical clues I'd have been able to pick up on the wards. Occasionally there are problems with the system, but you're never left with a blank screen, and because we're a national service there's always somebody else who can take a call. The most common calls are about coughs and colds, things people can manage on their own, but I need to look out for anything that will indicate that they might need to go and see a doctor. People can be embarrassed to go to hospital about minor ailments, but we often have to reassure them if it's the right thing to do.

C Agnes Thomson: broadcasting company

Yesterday I got lots of calls relating to weekly programmes, like there's a consumer programme and people generally call me because they have a problem with a product from a company we've covered on the show. We have regular callers, some very nice and some not so nice, and you get to know them. Quite often, people phone to complain spontaneously, and when we call them again within ten days with a response, which we promise to do in some cases, they've forgotten what made them cross. Television programmes probably generate more calls, particularly medical programmes or programmes about children. People have a sense that we're a general repository of knowledge and wisdom – which we're not! There'll have been a show that has covered most things at one time or another, so I can always look things up. As a result, I have a lot of what you might call useless knowledge.

D Caroline Hickman: household products company

I really get a lot out of the work. We have such a wide range of products – from beauty and haircare through to nappies and household cleaners – that no two calls are ever the same. With laundry products, for example, we get lots of specific queries – people want to know what to use with certain types of material. We also get a lot of calls about skin care from people who want to know about specific ingredients in our products. You also get fascinating insight into the country's lifestyles. For instance, we tend to get lots of calls about cleaning products on a Monday, presumably because people buy them over the weekend, then, towards Friday we'll get hair care and beauty because they're planning a night out. I also long for one-off problems I can really get my teeth into – the ones that come out of blue. We once had a call from a woman who'd seen a wedding dress on one of our TV adverts and wanted one identical to it for her own big day. We found that it was still at the television studio and was available for her to borrow – which she did. It just goes to show that it's always worth asking!

Part 1

You must answer this question. Write your answer in **220 – 260** words in an appropriate style.

In the exam, you write your answer **on a separate answer sheet**.

---

1   Your class has listened to a debate about the importance of competitive sport for young people. You have made the notes below:

> **Effect of competitive sport on young people**
> - builds confidence
> - creates pressure
> - provides enjoyment

> Some opinions expressed in the discussion:
>
> "I've never felt so silly as when I lost a match really badly."
>
> "I find that new challenges give me energy."
>
> "It's no fun when people treat a game very seriously."

Write an essay discussing **two** of the ways in your notes that sport can affect young people. You should **explain which effect is most important**, **giving reasons** to support your opinion.

You may, if you wish, make use of the opinions expressed in the discussion, but you should use your own words as far as possible.

Part 2

Write an answer to **one** of the questions **2 – 4** in this part. Write your answer in **220 – 260** words in an appropriate style. In the exam, you write your answer **on a separate answer sheet**, and put the question number in the box at the top of the page.

2   You have recently been on a long flight when you saw this announcement in the in-flight magazine.

> ### Reviews wanted!
> We're trying to add films to our in-flight entertainment, and we'd like reviews of films that you think are particularly impressive. They don't need to be new films!
>
> Write us a review of a film you think was impressive, describing what it's about, how it impressed you and explaining why you would recommend it for our in-flight entertainment package.

Write your **review**.

3   You see this announcement in an international travel magazine.

> **Have you had an exciting or unusual holiday?** For example, have you ever sailed anywhere on your own, gone rock climbing or camped anywhere out of the way? We'd like to hear about it! Write us a letter telling us where you went and why, what you did and how you felt about it afterwards. Has it affected you in any way?
>
> We'll publish the most interesting letters in our next edition.

Write your **letter**.

4   Your college wants to extend the facilities it provides for students to eat during the day, and has asked students for proposals for the best way to do this.

Write a proposal outlining the existing facilities, explaining why they need extending, and making recommendations for ways to improve these facilities for all students.

Write your **proposal**.

Part 1

You will hear three different extracts. For questions **1 – 6**, choose the answer (**A**, **B** or **C**) which fits best according to what you hear. There are two questions for each extract.

In the exam, you write your answers on **a separate answer sheet**.

Extract One

You hear part of an interview with a young actor called Sean.

1   Looking back, he admits that as a teenage TV star he was

   A   too immature to make the right decisions.
   B   dissatisfied with the work he was doing.
   C   foolish to give up a well-paid acting job.

2   What does he suggest about his current acting work?

   A   He's very selective in the roles he accepts.
   B   He's still playing some stereotypical roles.
   C   He's fortunate to be offered such a variety of roles.

Extract Two

You hear two radio editors talking about their work.

3   What do they agree about editing what a person has said?

   A   Your first priority is accuracy.
   B   It's important to include some imperfections.
   C   You shouldn't get to close to the person concerned.

4   What does the man suggest about the woman's voice?

   A   It has changed in quality over the years.
   B   It is still not an ideal one for radio work.
   C   It would be quite acceptable on radio now.

Extract Three

You hear part of a podcast about Africa.

5   What does the man do for a living?

   A   He writes.
   B   He organises trips.
   C   He works for a charity.

6   What does he say about development projects in Africa?

   A   He saw little evidence of their effects.
   B   He acknowledges that they play an important role.
   C   He accepts that local projects need international support.

Part 2

You will hear a journalist, called Stella Faulds, talking about why some people seem to be naturally clumsy. For questions **7 – 14**, complete the sentences with a word or short phrase.

In the exam, you mark your answers **on a separate answer sheet**.

Clumsiness

Stella sees no connection between being clumsy and

(7) .... or other abilities in life.

The book where Stella read a description of a clumsy person was a

(8) ....

Stella mentions both **(9)** .... and ....

as outdoor places where her relative's clumsiness became apparent.

Stella is often complemented on her **(10)** ....

as well as her speed in certain skills.

Stella admits to feeling **(11)** ....

when her brother, Adam, plays tennis well.

Adam has a family reputation for having what they call **(12)** ....

Stella describes how Adam recently got a **(13)** ....

caught in an escalator.

Stella wonders if a lack of **(14)** ....

could explain her clumsiness.

Part 3

You will hear part of an interview with a woman called Barbara Darby who works as a casting director in the film industry. For questions **15 – 20**, choose the answer (**A, B, C** or **D**) which fits best according to what you hear.

In the exam, write your answers **on a separate answer sheet**.

---

15 According to Barbara, a casting director needs, above all,

- **A** to learn from experience.
- **B** to be a good communicator.
- **C** to have a relevant qualification.
- **D** to have a natural feel for the job.

16 Barbara says that she looks for actors who

- **A** can play a variety of roles.
- **B** complement each other.
- **C** accept her way of working.
- **D** think deeply about a part.

17 At which stage in the casting process does Barbara meet the actors?

- **A** Before she goes to see them performing live.
- **B** Once the director has approved them.
- **C** Before a final short-list is drawn up.
- **D** As soon as a final selection is made.

18 What led Barbara to become a casting director?

- **A** She was doing similar work in the theatre.
- **B** She realised she had the skills needed.
- **C** It was recommended by a colleague.
- **D** It had always been her ambition.

19 Barbara explains that what motivates her now is a need for

- **A** personal satisfaction.
- **B** professional recognition.
- **C** a glamorous lifestyle.
- **D** financial security.

20 What made Barbara give up her job for a while?

- **A** She'd become tired of travelling.
- **B** She was ready to try something new.
- **C** She felt she'd been put under too much pressure.
- **D** She found that she was no longer as committed to it.

LISTENING **TEST 5**

TEST 5

LISTENING

Part 4

You will hear five short extracts in which people are talking about vehicles they own.
In the exam, mark your answers **on a separate answer sheet**.

TASK ONE

For questions **21 – 25**, choose from the list (**A – H**) what led each speaker to buy the type of vehicle they own.

TASK TWO

For questions **26 – 30**, choose from the list (**A – H**) why each speaker feels satisfied with their vehicle now.

While you listen you must complete both tasks.

A	its individuality	**A**	It allows me to live by my principles.
B	a frustrating delay	**B**	It's a way of impressing clients.
C	economic necessity	**C**	It keeps me on schedule.
D	some surplus income	**D**	It helps me cope with challenges at work.
E	a special offer	**E**	It means I can continue a family tradition.
F	its mechanical simplicity	**F**	It reflects my own love of speed.
G	the type of fuel it uses	**G**	It's allowed me to increase my workload.
H	an uncomfortable commute	**H**	It suits my feelings of nostalgia.

Speaker 1 [ ] 21
Speaker 2 [ ] 22
Speaker 3 [ ] 23
Speaker 4 [ ] 24
Speaker 5 [ ] 25

Speaker 1 [ ] 26
Speaker 2 [ ] 27
Speaker 3 [ ] 28
Speaker 4 [ ] 29
Speaker 5 [ ] 30

Part 1 (2 minutes)

The examiner will ask you one or two questions about yourself and what you think about everyday topics such as work or study, travel, holidays, daily life and routines. For example:

- What do you enjoy most about visiting other countries? (Why?)
- What kind of books do you usually read for pleasure? (Why?)
- If you could be really good at one sport, what would it be?

Part 2 (4 minutes)

Turn to the pictures on page 182, which show **people and animals**.

PEOPLE AND ANIMALS

Candidate A, I'd like you to compare **two** of the pictures, and say **why the animals might be important to the people, and how the people might be feeling**.

Candidate B, **who do you think will have the longest relationship with the animals? (Why?)**

GETTING AROUND

Turn to the pictures on page 184, which show people getting around in different ways.

Candidate B, compare **two** of the pictures and say **why the people might have chosen to get around in these ways, and why their journey might be important to them**.

Candidate A, **who do you think will remember their journey the longest? (Why?)**

Part 3 (4 minutes)

Turn to the diagram on page 183, which shows some things that many people think indicate a successful life.

Now, talk to each other about **how far these things indicate a successful life**.

Now decide **which one is the best indication of a successful life**.

Part 4 (5 minutes)

Answer these questions.

- What does success mean for you? (Why?)
- Some people say it's not important to be successful, it's better to be happy. What do you think? Why?
- Do you think that people are too concerned about being successful these days? (Why / Why not?)
- Some people are not at all ambitious. Is this a bad thing? (Why / Why not?)
- What do you think drives sports people to try to be champions? (Why?)
- Some people, like artists or composers, are only recognised after their death. Why do you think this is?

SPEAKING **TEST 5**

TEST 6

Part 1

For questions **1 – 8**, read the text below and decide which answer (**A, B, C** or **D**) best fits each gap. There is an example at the beginning (**0**).

In the exam, you mark your answers **on a separate answer sheet**.

Example:
0   A amount   B quantity   C volume   D extent

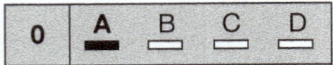

A question of safety

Life involves a certain **(0)** .... of risk, or at least it did. These days, however, governments seem to have become **(1)** .... with the idea of protecting us from it. As a result, what we actually risk most is not being allowed to live at all.

One edict, which emerged from the British government's health-and-safety department, would be amusing if it wasn't so serious. Circus artistes performing on tightropes or the flying trapeze are being **(2)** .... to wear the type of hard hats more usually **(3)** .... with the construction industry. Under the 'Temporary Work at Heights Directive', such a hat must be worn for any working activity taking **(4)** .... above the height of an 'average stepladder'. Now you might think that sounds **(5)** .... reasonable, but the absurd thing is that the rule is being **(6)** .... to circus performers as well. Used to flying through the air without even the **(7)** .... of a safety net, performers point out that trapeze artistes often break arms and legs, but **(8)** .... heads.

1	A prone	B obsessed	C addicted	D devoted
2	A proposed	B challenged	C required	D demanded
3	A regarded	B associated	C recognised	D concerned
4	A place	B forth	C part	D ahead
5	A fairly	B duly	C widely	D closely
6	A presided	B enforced	C directed	D applied
7	A profit	B benefit	C remedy	D welfare
8	A merely	B unlikely	C rarely	D unusually

Part 2

For questions **9 – 16**, read the text below and think of the word which best fits each gap. Use only **one** word in each gap. There is an example at the beginning (**0**).

In the exam, you write your answers **IN CAPITAL LETTERS on a separate answer sheet.**

Example: 0 N O

The hamster's body clock

Hamsters have **(0)** .... need for alarm clocks. In the strange world of circadian rhythms – the 24-hour cycle **(9)** .... governs almost every biological process in every living thing, **(10)** .... body temperature to digestion to sleeping and waking – the hamster is **(11)** .... equivalent of the Swiss watch. **(12)** .... to Professor Michael Antle from the University of Calgary's Department of Psychology, you can predict to within a minute **(13)** .... a hamster is going to wake up.

(14) .... turning on their light for 15 minutes in the middle of the night, however, he can make his hamsters wake up an hour earlier the next day. They still need their usual fourteen hours' sleep, but their biological clocks appear to be set back. When he saw the effect initially in his laboratory, Antle was shocked at **(15)** .... big it was. An eight-hour adjustment is something useful – it could mean travelling from Canada to London without suffering from jetlag. **(16)** .... the same thing worked for humans, Antle really would be on to something.

Part 3

For questions **17 – 24**, read the text below. Use the word given in capitals at the end of some of the lines to form a word that fits in the gap **in the same line**. There is an example at the beginning (**0**).

In the exam, you write your answers **IN CAPITAL LETTERS on a separate answer sheet**.

Example: | 0 | E | S | S | E | N | T | I | A | L | L | Y | | | |

Intrepid travel

Intrepid Travel is **(0)** ………. a tour operator which aims to provide **ESSENCE**
its clients with holidays that take them off the **(17)** ………. track in small **BEAT**
groups, whilst at the same time allowing them the **(18)** ………. and **FLEXIBLE**
freedom to really gain first-hand experience of local cultures.

The company divides trips into two categories. The Active Range
aims to combine physical challenge with cultural **(19)** ………. , **INTERACT**
whereas the Comfort Range puts the emphasis more on a **(20)** ………. **COMBINE**
of travel to unusual destinations and some of life's small **(21)** ………. . **PLEASE**
In other words, you have a **(22)** ………. of intrepid adventures to suit **CHOOSE**
both your budget and your preferred level of comfort.

For example, you might find a trek in Peru more to your taste than,
say, a feast in Morocco; or maybe an African safari is more likely
to meet your **(23)** ………. . Intrepid clients get the chance to see **REQUIRE**
some of the world's most amazing places, engage with fascinating
cultures and have some **(24)** ………. real-life experiences along the way. **FORGET**

Part 4

For questions **25 – 30**, complete the second sentence so that it has a similar meaning to the first sentence, using the word given. **Do not change the word given**. You must use between **three** and **six** words, including the word given. Here is an example (**0**).

Example:

0   Chloe would only eat a pizza if she could have a mushroom topping.
ON
Chloe .... a mushroom topping when she ate a pizza.

The gap can be filled with the words 'insisted on having', so you write:

Example: | 0 | INSISTED ON HAVING

In the exam, you write **only** the missing words **IN CAPITAL LETTERS on a separate answer sheet**.

---

25   Leo is so skilful at basketball that he makes it look easy.
IS
Such .... basketball player that he makes it look easy.

26   Brian couldn't explain how the stolen computer got into the boot of his car.
LOSS
Brian .... how the stolen computer got into the boot of his car.

27   The footballer injured his knee, so that was the end of his hopes of a first team place.
PAID
The footballer's knee .... his hopes of a first team place.

28   This film stands a very good chance of winning an award.
HIGHLY
It is .... win an award.

29   Davina can't even boil an egg and she certainly couldn't cook a whole meal.
ALONE
Davina can't even boil an egg .... a whole meal

30   Kelvin should call in a builder to repair those broken roof tiles.
GET
Kevin should .... by a builder.

Part 5

You are going to read an article about privacy. For questions **31 – 36**, choose the answer (**A**, **B**, **C** or **D**) which you think fits best according to the text.

In the exam, you mark your answers **on a separate answer sheet**.

All the world's her stage

The concept of the Renaissance man or woman, someone who has acquired success or proficiency in several fields, holds a deep appeal in our multi-tasking present. This, after all, is the age of the juggler. Given the limitless opportunities available in our complex society, the notion of pursuing just one career seems a bit pedestrian. Antonia Campbell Hughes, who starred on the Dublin stage in the play *Roberto Zucco*, appears to be the consummate Renaissance woman. Into her short career she has crammed stints as a fashion designer (flogging frocks both under her own name and as part of a diffusion line for the retail chain Topshop), a Paris catwalk model and a star of the big and small screens.

The industries in which Campbell Hughes chooses to work may seem disparate, but they have one trait in common: glamour. She may, perhaps, be a member of the slasher brigade: an actress-slash-model-slash-designer who is eager for fame and happy to pursue any route to its attainment. The key distinction between the Renaissance woman and the slasher is devotion to one's pursuits. So is Antonia a dilettante or devotee?

The woman herself insists that her careers have flowed organically from each other. "People never really see the connection between fashion and drama, but I think there's a huge connection. I saw fashion as creating a scene and a setting and characters, building the entire cast effectively. All my collections were always about creating a mood and an atmosphere and a character. Fashion seemed the most direct avenue. I never understood how people who are creative are satisfied with one outlet, one medium. I always did all kinds of things. In Paris, we didn't have enough money to do catwalk shows, so we'd take gallery spaces and set up a soiree-type thing. You put the various pieces on mannequins and have installation videos and all that kind of vibe. I'd do favours for friends as well and act in their videos."

Antonia was born in Derry, in the west of Ireland, but her parents left the country when she was two, and she grew up in Switzerland and the US. She moved to Dublin in her mid-teens but didn't find the school syllabus particularly absorbing. "I didn't go much. I was very much a rebellious teen, and I wanted to sing in bands and travel the world and be away from my normal environment. I thought art school was the best avenue, so I went to New York for a bit and got into fashion."

Her move into acting was almost accidental. "A man called John McGuire stopped me on the street and asked me to do a music video, some little kind of ambient trip-hop thing," she says. "That made me quite uncertain as to which avenue I was going down. From there I very much fell into television, into comedy. I just went for an audition and got a part in a TV sitcom; I never had a hankering to do British TV and didn't know much about the show. But I think the comedy field in British television is quite strong, and I really respect the producer's work and it's such a lovely programme to work on. It's very scripted, but the writers are open to suggestion. If things crop up on the day, they're very much incorporated, which is a lovely way to work."

In person, Antonia comes across as charmingly childlike, continually fidgeting and changing conversational tack mid-sentence. This impression is compounded by her elfin appearance – few might guess she has been on the planet for a quarter-century. She's happy to play up this image, and has been known to spend parties sitting under tables, affecting a girlish blitheness. This insouciance, contrived or otherwise, does not prevent her from worrying about being typecast as a comic artist. "I wanted to do this play because it's a completely different approach from comedy."

31 In the first paragraph, the writer suggests that

- **A** it may be unwise to try out too many different careers.
- **B** people who are very focussed on one career may appear dull.
- **C** to succeed in life you need to learn a range of complex skills.
- **D** a wide range of work experience is good training for an actress.

32 The writer uses the term 'slasher brigade' (line **17**)

- **A** to suggest how acting and fashion have a lot in common.
- **B** to emphasise how versatile people like Antonia have to be.
- **C** to show where he thinks Antonia's true motivation comes from.
- **D** to describe people who may lack Antonia's level of commitment.

33 When talking about her work as a fashion designer, Antonia is explaining

- **A** how financial necessity led her to seek acting work.
- **B** why it was impossible to get her designs noticed.
- **C** how she approached the creation of a collection.
- **D** why she found the profession unsatisfying.

34 How did Antonia feel whilst at school in Dublin?

- **A** unsure about the type of education she needed
- **B** unstimulated by what she was expected to study
- **C** unsettled by her educational experiences elsewhere
- **D** disappointed by the way creative subjects were taught

35 What does Antonia say about her decision to do television work in Britain?

- **A** She was attracted to it by the opportunities to improvise.
- **B** She liked the fact that the actors also write the scripts.
- **C** It was the kind of thing she had always wanted to try.
- **D** It was something that she got into almost by chance.

36 What does the phrase 'This insouciance' (line **67**) refer to?

- **A** Antonia's apparently carefree attitude
- **B** Antonia's professional reputation
- **C** Antonia's physical appearance
- **D** Antonia's way of speaking

Part 6

You are going to read four extracts from reports written by people who attended a conference on the subject of innovation in business. For questions **37 – 40**, choose from the extracts **A – D**. The extracts may be chosen more than once.

In the exam, you mark your answers **on a separate answer sheet.**

A Alec Royle

I spent a stimulating three days at the conference entitled 'Managing Successful innovation'. This brought together under one roof almost 500 managers who, as one presenter aptly put it: "recognise the need to encourage innovation, but don't always know how to achieve it". Innovation is indeed a hot topic just now, and at this event it was thoroughly dissected from a variety of angles by some accomplished speakers. Given that we were at a hotel with state-of-the-art, purpose-built conference facilities including comfortable lecture theatres and spacious public areas, it's a shame more time wasn't built in for informal mingling with the other attendees – always such a valuable part of these events. You couldn't fault the refreshments, however. Short as the breaks were, there was a ready supply of intriguing snacks on offer. It was as if the hotel kitchen had been asked to pick up on the theme of the conference itself.

B Ben Wong

As a seasoned conference-goer, I find myself paying less attention to who's been paid to speak than to who's being paid to go and listen. That, for me, is the real benefit of events like last month's conference on innovation in business, and I did come away with a pocketful of calling cards. I've already started chasing up the most promising ones. It was also heartening to see so many other managers sharing my views on the significance of innovation, and the need to promote it to survive in our fast-changing commercial environment. Of the formal sessions, none came close to matching the energy and originality of some of those at last year's event, when the focus was on disruptive technology. A theme unintentionally revisited this year when a hitch in the kitchen meant half the items on the lunch menu never materialised.

C Chris Shakeston

I'd been told that this conference centre was the hot ticket in terms of what the hospitality industry has to offer – so it was a bit of a let-down to find the catering was a bit run-of-the-mill. Innovation is certainly a buzzword in the business community, so Managing Successful Innovation seemed a promising conference to sign up for. But I came away thinking that the current 'era of innovation' as I heard it described is a bit of an exaggeration. In reality, developing new concepts and inventions is what humans have always done. Admittedly, there were some very polished talks by world-renowned management gurus, but the main thrust of the programme seemed a bit hackneyed to me. Conferences are about building relationships as well as provoking thought, however, and strengthening such bonds and extending our reach is the real reason many of us were there.

D Dan Gomez

I've been to lots of conferences in my time – some excellent and some less so. The recent one I attended on the subject of Managing Successful Innovation wasn't the worst, but neither was it the best I've known. There were some famous names on the programme and the sessions were certainly slick in terms of delivery. The issue for me, however, was that so much has been said on the subject in recent years that even these well-known practitioners in the field of innovation had little to add. Judging by the chat over the rather uninspiring lunch, I wasn't alone in feeling that innovation was precisely what seemed to be in short supply! To my mind, there was also a bit too much input on the packed programme. I'd have appreciated more time for interacting with the other participants and getting to know a few people. Isn't that why we go to conferences?

Which attendee

shares Ben Wong's opinion about the relevance of the overall theme of the conference? 37 ☐

has a different view to the other three regarding the performance of the presenters at the conference? 38 ☐

shares Alec Royle's view of the opportunities for networking at the conference? 39 ☐

has a different opinion to Chris Shakeston about the catering arrangements at the conference? 40 ☐

Part 7

You are going to read an extract from a magazine. Six paragraphs have been removed from the article. Choose from the paragraphs **A – G** the one which fits each gap (**41 – 46**). There is one extra paragraph which you do not need to use.

In the exam, you mark your answers **on a separate answer sheet**.

Life choices

Would you give up a dull but secure job to fulfil your ream ambition? Susannah Bates did.

We last interviewed Susannah Bates five years ago, just after the publication of her second novel in little more than 12 months. And then it went a bit quiet. Her third tale is now out – so why the long gap? Well, we need to rewind to January six years ago. In that month, Susannah rekindled a romance with a former boyfriend from her days at university. Her first book, *Charmed Lives*, was out not long after – and pretty quickly, it seems life was imitating art.

41

The sequel, also featuring a city lawyer, was by this time pretty much done and dusted and would appear on the bookshelves the following spring. "I'd already done a bit of work on the next one, but not a huge amount. But when I did get down to working on it, it didn't come as easily as the others. They came out quite quickly, and then there's been this gap."

42

The successful publication of three novels, with one to come as part of her current publishing deal, certainly vindicates her decision to turn her back on the law after two years at law school, and a year working in London. Wisdom is about realising what works for you, and she hasn't looked back.

43

"What's more, when I was trying to get published and taken on by an agent, I was treated more seriously because I was a lawyer; I suspect because it shows you can put your head down and do hard work. But I eventually decided I just wasn't temperamentally suited to it. I came to specialise in banking law. They didn't ever say you had to be that good with numbers, but I think it would've helped!" she laughs.

44

"Those who stay in the industry do it because they love that side of it. They get a real buzz and think 'This deal's worth eight million' or 'The deal we're working on is going to be on the front pages of the business section.' For me, it could have been eight dollars. Eight million? It wasn't that big an issue. It didn't give me the same thrill."

45

"I've never thought writing was a realistic option, especially my sort of writing, because so many people fail at it. Maybe it's my upbringing, but I really felt it was important, leaving university, to earn money, and I didn't see how I could ever do that by writing. I think that was the real explanation, and I wanted to be independent. I also thought that whatever I did, I'd put my head down and come to enjoy it; I didn't realise I'd find the law quite so dry!"

46

But that's all in the past. Thoughts for the future centre on a fourth novel. There's no title as yet, but there are many thoughts swirling and settling in Susannah's mind.

A "I was incredibly naïve to think that initial feeling would change, and I took a while to realise I was hitting my head against a brick wall. Maybe it was because there's part of me that likes ticking boxes and jumping through hoops and getting approval, and there's a lot of that in the law."

B It features a successful high-flying young lawyer who has everything except a life outside the office, until she meets her beau. Susannah was a lawyer who gave up the law in order to write, and who then met hers. They got engaged as spring turned into summer, and before the end of the year, were married.

C "It's as if I suddenly saw the light," she says. "I've got a friend from that time and I hate to think what he's earning compared to what I'm earning! But I don't really regret giving it up. I don't regret having done it, either; I think it's really great grounding, knowing what it is to be a professional, and I've used aspects of that in my writing."

D "My mother's quite realistic about decisions and I remember her saying when I was wondering whether to go through with it: 'Write a short story, send it to a magazine, see how it gets on.'"

E To an outsider, therefore, it seems a bit surprising that Susannah joined the profession in the first place. As an English student at university, she co-wrote a couple of plays, performed at a national festival; one was nominated for an award. So why didn't she follow a literary star?

F That department appealed because she liked the amusing people there. "You could have fun flicking elastic bands at everyone or sending a fake email from someone else's computer, but at the end of the day you had to go back to your desk and look at those rows of figures," she smiles.

G "When I'm working on a novel, I need to shut myself away. It's quite a sad, lonely activity," she laughs. "But when life's looking up and you're busy and have someone around, you're very easily distracted. It took a long time to find my rhythm again."

Part 8

You are going to read an article about the sport called canyoning. For questions **47 – 56**, choose from the designers (**A – D**). The sections may be chosen more than once.

In the exam, you mark your answers **on a separate answer sheet**.

Which section mentions

a variant of the sport that is less challenging?	47
a way of mastering the basic skills required by the sport?	48
an example of why the sport demands both courage and determination?	49
artificial aids that have been introduced for the benefit of participants?	50
a growing awareness of the sport in certain places?	51
how some of the best locations for the sport were discovered?	52
a specially adapted piece of gear that is available to participants?	53
the type of people who pioneered the sport?	54
the aim of each canyoning expedition?	55
professional guidance in obtaining the most appropriate equipment?	56

Gorge yourself

A

After a long, hard week crunching numbers, writing up reports, doing assignments or whatever it is you do, don't you sometimes feel like chucking yourself off a cliff? Well, you're not alone. There's even a name for people with such impulses: they're called canyoneers. Canyoning, which was established as a sport around 15 years ago by a few fearless thrill-seekers in France and Spain, is being adopted as the latest way for stressed-out high achievers to purge themselves of the pressures of work or study – for the simple reason that nothing clears the mind better than the prospect of leaping off the side of a gorge into a pool of limpid, mountain-fresh water which can be as much as 20 metres beneath your feet. There is, however, more to canyoning than that: it's a true adventure sport that regularly embraces the disciplines of hiking, climbing, abseiling and swimming, and it's certainly not for the faint of heart or weak of limb.

B

A typical canyoneers outfit costs around £1,250 and comprises a high-quality wetsuit, neoprene socks and gloves, a safety helmet fitted with a waterproof headlight and a perforated canyoning backpack designed to let out all the weighty water that accumulates on the way down. You'll also need a decent first-aid kit (just in case) and top-notch climbing equipment including ropes and a harness and last but not least, a few equally adventurous friends. Because if there's one thing canyoning isn't, it's a sport for the lone wolf. Although it's difficult to define precisely, canyoning basically involves making your way to the top of an extremely long and high gorge and then traversing your way down to the bottom by the best means possible – which usually involves a combination of abseiling, climbing, jumping, sliding and swimming. One thing it always requires, however, is commitment – because once you're halfway down a creek it's often far more difficult to turn back and try to reach the safety of flat terrain than it is to keep on going. Even though going on might involve an abseil down a sheer rock face or a seemingly interminable creep around a ledge barely 15 centimetres wide.

C

In the early days it was very much a voyage of discovery, with pioneering canyoneers seeking out interesting-looking gorges and simply going for it to see if there was a navigable route from top to bottom. Since then, however, many of those gorges have been opened up by professional guides who have established safer, but still exciting, routes and have also equipped the rocks with climbing bolts, hooks and rings to which visiting canyoneers can rope up. Typical of the type of people who are becoming hooked on the sport is Christine Pasquier, who works in the luxury goods industry. "When I started about 15 years ago it didn't have a name and it wasn't regarded as a sport," she says. "It just involved people walking through fairly shallow canyons, usually without any protective clothing. About eight years ago, however, it really began to develop, particularly in France and Spain, where everyone now recognises the word 'canyoning'".

D

If the thought of spending an entire day getting exhausted and soaking wet and frightening yourself silly appeals, the first step into canyoning is to get some expert training. Firms such as Espace Evasion will not only guide you through some of Europe's most breathtakingly beautiful canyons, they'll also provide you with all the gear and teach you all the essential roping, abseiling and descent techniques to get you started. If you're UK-based, however, there are various organisations that offer the opportunity to have a go at canyoning and a similar activity called gorge walking, which is a drier version of canyoning. In neither case will the experience be as dramatic or thrilling as you will find at a location such as Sierra de Guara in Spain, but at least you'll have a chance to discover that canyoning is not for you – or, more likely, that you think it's simply gorgeous.

Part 1

You must answer this question. Write your answer in **220 – 260** words in an appropriate style.

In the exam, write your answer **on a separate answer sheet**.

1   Your class has taken part in a debate on the kind of role models young people look up to, and why they might be important. You have made the notes below:

> **Role models – who should they be and why?**
> - parents
> - celebrities
> - sports people
>
> Some opinions expressed in the discussion:
>
> "My parents were great when I was young, but now they're a bit out of touch."
>
> "Celebrities are great because we can all aspire to their lifestyles."
>
> "The way sports people face challenges is so inspiring."

Write an essay discussing **two** of the kinds of role models in your notes who can affect young people. You should **explain which kind of role model is most important for young people**, **giving reasons** to support your opinion.

You may, if you wish, make use of the opinions expressed in the discussion, but you should use your own words as far as possible.

Part 2

Write an answer to **one** of the questions **2 – 4** in this part. Write your answer in **220 – 260** words in an appropriate style. In the exam, you write your answer **on a separate answer sheet**, and put the question number in the box at the top of the page.

2   The college where you study English has a study centre where students can work by themselves in the evenings. This centre has not been used much recently, and the principal wants to know why.

Write a report for the principal, outlining the situation and making recommendations for ways of encouraging students to use the study centre more.

Write your **report**.

3   You see this announcement on a shopping website:

> We know you all like video games, and we'd like you to share those that you've found especially good.
>
> Write us a review of your favourite game, saying whether it's easy for anyone to play, why you like it and whether you would recommend it for players of all ages. We'll publish the most useful reviews on our website.

Write your **review**.

4   Your town has organised an English-language club that meets every Thursday evening, and wants to attract new members. The organisers have asked residents for proposals to increase the membership of the club.

Write a proposal outlining the current situation and aims of the club, suggesting activities the club could provide and recommending other ways of encouraging people to join.

Write your **proposal**.

Part 1

You will hear three different extracts. For questions **1 – 6**, choose the answer (**A, B** or **C**) which fits best according to what you hear. There are two questions for each extract.

In the exam, you write your answers **on a seperate answer sheet**.

Extract One

You hear two radio presenters talking about a new music album.

1   They agree that the music on the album

   A   is very atmospheric.
   B   is occasionally over sentimental.
   C   is very sophisticated given the age of the band.

2   The man feels that this type of music

   A   is better heard live.
   B   is reminiscent of a film soundtrack.
   C   is best listened to at a certain time of day.

Extract Two

You hear the beginning of a podcast about interior design.

3   According to the male presenter, a home office should

   A   take up as little space as possible.
   B   be both practical and stylish in appearance.
   C   not be located in an area used for relaxation.

4   What is Debbie Brewer doing?

   A   recommending a useful piece of furniture
   B   reviewing the latest technological innovations
   C   advising on the most effective storage systems

Extract Three

You will hear part of a travel programme about a destination for a weekend city break.

5   In the woman's opinion, the main advantage of visiting the city is

   A   its proximity to an airport.
   B   the simplicity of the facilities.
   C   the quality of local produce.

6   What possible disadvantage does the man warn us about?

   A   the inadequate nature of the public transport
   B   the high incidence of petty crime
   C   the complicated street plan

Part 2

You will hear part of a lecture by the geographer Wendy Mason who is talking about Antarctica. For questions **7 – 14**, complete the sentences with a word or short phrase.

In the exam, mark your answers **on a separate answer sheet**.

Antarctica

Wendy says that as many as **(7)** .... countries have research bases in Antarctica.

Wendy says that some people regard polar research as both overrated and too **(8)** ....

Antarctica's largest settlement is the US base which most people call **(9)** ....

Only scientists and their **(10)** .... may use flights landing at the US base.

Near the US base, there are some **(11)** .... built by 20th-century explorers.

Most tourists visiting Antarctica go to an area of **(12)** .... and ....

A private company built the **(13)** .... as well as a camp in the Patriot Hills.

Wendy uses the word **(14)** .... to describe the type of tourism that would not pollute Antarctica.

Part 3

You will hear part of an interview in which a young artist called Lynda Buckland is talking about her life and work. For questions **15 – 20**, choose the answer (**A, B, C** or **D**) which fits best according to what you hear.

In the exam, you write your answers **on a separate answer sheet**.

---

15 Lynda says that she chooses to draw river scenes because

    A   you find interesting characters there.
    B   the surrounding landscape inspires her.
    C   it's a theme that's instantly recognisable.
    D   she likes their feeling of dynamic activity.

16 What is Lynda's attitude towards abstract art?

    A   She doesn't want her work to go in that direction.
    B   She regrets not having moved into it earlier.
    C   She wishes she'd had more training in it.
    D   She's looking forward to trying it out.

17 Lynda says that she produces her final drawings

    A   whilst she's sitting on the waterfront itself.
    B   immediately after seeing the scenes which inspire her.
    C   after combining ideas from different sketches she's done.
    D   on days when she's able to rent space in a studio near the river.

18 What was the disadvantage of Lynda's previous workspace?

    A   It lacked atmosphere.
    B   It was affected by traffic noise.
    C   It was in an inconvenient location.
    D   It was larger than she actually needed.

19 How did Lynda find her new workspace?

    A   She met somebody by chance who had a studio to let.
    B   She saw evidence of artistic activity in a nearby building.
    C   She went to see it on the recommendation of a neighbour.
    D   She was invited to join a group of artists working in her area.

20 Lynda says that the drawings on show in her forthcoming exhibition

    A   took longer to produce than some of her earlier work.
    B   represent a mix of her latest work and older material.
    C   include features that reflect recent changes in her life.
    D   contain signs of how her work will change in the future.

TEST 6 LISTENING

Part 4

You will hear five short extracts in which people are talking about weekend breaks they have been on recently.

In the exam, mark your answers **on a separate answer sheet**.

TASK ONE

For questions **21 – 25**, choose from the list (**A – H**) the type of activity each speaker did on their weekend break.

TASK TWO

For questions **26 – 30**, choose from the list (**A – H**) what each speaker says they disliked about their weekend break.

While you listen you must complete both tasks.

A	hill-walking
B	fishing
C	bird-watching
D	sailing
E	windsurfing
F	cycling
G	horse-riding
H	rock-climbing

Speaker 1 21
Speaker 2 22
Speaker 3 23
Speaker 4 24
Speaker 5 25

A	the choice at mealtimes
B	the attitude of the staff
C	the sleeping arrangements
D	the quality of the equipment
E	the evening entertainment
F	other participants
G	unexpected costs
H	how things were scheduled

Speaker 1 26
Speaker 2 27
Speaker 3 28
Speaker 4 29
Speaker 5 30

Part 1 (2 minutes)

The examiner will ask you one or two questions about yourself and what you think about everyday topics such as work or study, travel, holidays, daily life and routines.

- Is there something you'd like to be really good at? (Why?)
- What would you like to be doing in two years' time? (Why?)
- Apart from English, is there a language you'd like to learn? (Why / Why not?)

Part 2 (4 minutes)

Turn to the pictures on page 185, which show **people studying in different situations**.

PEOPLE STUDYING

Candidate A, I'd like you to compare **two** of the pictures, and say **why the people might have chosen to study in these different places and how important it might be for them to be able to concentrate on their studies**.

Candidate B, **who do you think feels that it's important to study well? (Why?)**

ENTERTAINING OTHERS

Turn to the pictures on page 186, which show people entertaining others.

Candidate B, compare **two** of the pictures and say **how easy it might be to entertain others in these situations, and how important it might be to perform well**.

Candidate A, **who do you think has the most difficult task? (Why?)**

Part 3 (4 minutes)

Turn to the diagram on page 187, which shows ways in which the media affects our lives.

Now, talk to each other about **the benefits and drawbacks of the ways in which the media affects our lives**.

Now decide **which impact of the media is the most beneficial for everyone**.

Part 4 (5 minutes)

Answer these questions.

- In your opinion, what's the best way to find out about the news – television, newspapers or the internet? (Why?)
- Some people say the media tends to focus on bad news. Why is this?
- Do you think celebrities should be associated with the advertising of any products or brands? (Why / Why not?)
- What changes would you like to see take place in the media? (Why?)
- Do you think that people have lost the ability to entertain themselves because of the availability of the media? (Why / Why not?)
- Do you think people trust the media more or less than in the past? (Why?)

TEST 7

Part 1

For questions **1 – 8**, read the text below and decide which answer (**A, B, C** or **D**) best fits each gap. There is an example at the beginning (**0**).

In the exam, you mark your answers **on a separate answer sheet**.

Example:
0   A affecting   B occurring   C impinging   D relating

| 0 | **A** ▬ | B ▢ | C ▢ | D ▢ |

Expedition health

Sprains and muscle strains are common injuries **(0)** .... people who go trekking in wilderness areas. Ankles, knees, the larger leg muscles and the back are most at **(1)** .... especially if you're carrying a heavy backpack.

One way of avoiding these problems is to walk with trekking poles which help **(2)** .... balance as well as redistributing the shock load produced by constant walking.

Back strain can be triggered by the **(3)** .... of trekking and climbing, particularly when hamstrings are overused. To keep such strains at bay, take a few minutes at the end of each day to **(4)** .... these muscles. Lie on your back and hold your knees up against your chest. Then, keeping your knees together, roll your legs from side to side.

(5) .... treatment is concerned, you should **(6)** .... the temptation to reach straight for the drugs. Sprains and strains **(7)** .... from rest, ice compression and elevation. This combination of measures **(8)** .... the effect of reducing swelling and bruising.

1	**A** chance	**B** danger	**C** risk	**D** hazard
2	**A** supply	**B** maintain	**C** conserve	**D** defend
3	**A** rigours	**B** hardships	**C** sufferings	**D** ordeals
4	**A** spread	**B** extend	**C** stretch	**D** expand
5	**A** As far as	**B** As soon as	**C** As well as	**D** As long as
6	**A** resist	**B** defy	**C** restrain	**D** oppose
7	**A** improve	**B** recover	**C** respond	**D** benefit
8	**A** gives	**B** makes	**C** has	**D** gets

Part 2

For questions **9 – 16**, read the text below and think of the word which best fits each gap. Use only **one** word in each gap. There is an example at the beginning (**0**).

In the exam, you write your answers **IN CAPITAL LETTERS on a separate answer sheet**.

Example: **0** O N

The written word and the camera

Film isn't just about moving images and spoken language – the written word can also have a strong impact **(0)** ……… the big screen. In the first silent comedies and dramas, words emblazoned on a black screen helped audiences to understand **(9)** ……… they were seeing. Words spelled **(10)** ……… what the characters were saying, and connected the different scenes. For example, in between a scene showing our hero rushing to save his beloved and **(11)** ……… of her being tied to the train tracks, the word 'Meanwhile' **(12)** ……… invariably appear on the screen.

(13) ……… the introduction of sound made most of this wording redundant, the written word did not disappear from film. **(14)** ……… with the music, the design of the written title and opening credits helped to set the scene and establish the mood of the film. Film posters picked **(15)** ……… on this design feature, and became just as important as the artwork in attracting the right kind of audience to the film. A simple sheet of paper was turned **(16)** ……… an emotional experience equal to the film itself, with the lettering also playing a key role.

Part 3

For questions **17 – 24**, read the text below. Use the word given in capitals at the end of some of the lines to form a word that fits in the gap **in the same line**. There is an example at the beginning (**0**).

In the exam, you write your answers **IN CAPITAL LETTERS** on a separate answer sheet.

Example: 0 I D E N T I F Y

Hidden depths

Archaeologists have used aerial photography for many decades to (0) .... patterns of ancient human activity on the ground. Certain features of an area, such as ancient field boundaries or the outline of (17) .... and fortifications, which can no longer be seen on the ground, become (18) .... when viewed from above. The use of such photography has (19) .... archaeologists to produce maps of how the land has been used over the centuries. But these maps have always had gaps where the land is wooded because traditional cameras can't see through trees.

IDENTITY

SETTLE
APPEAR
ABLE

(20) ...., a solution to this problem has now been found. It's called Lidar, and it's a laser-based aerial (21) .... system that can 'see through' trees, thus revealing archaeological features concealed below. Lidar bounces low-energy laser pulses off the ground and measures how long it takes light to travel back to the instrument. Most of the pulses are from the trees, but some have reached the ground.

HAPPY
DETECT

A computer selects and (22) .... these and produces an image of the bare earth. Pioneering work with the technology led to the discovery of hundreds of previously (23) .... ancient features which tend to be (24) .... to the naked eye.

ANALYSIS

KNOW
VISIBLE

Part 4

For questions **25 – 30**, complete the second sentence so that it has a similar meaning to the first sentence, using the word given. **Do not change the word given.** You must use between **three** and **six** words, including the word given. Here is an example (**0**).

Example:

0   Trevor persuaded his sister to enter the competition.

   TALKED

   Trevor .... entering the competition.

The gap can be filled with the words 'talked his sister into', so you write:

Example: | 0 | TALKED HIS SISTER INTO |

In the exam, you write **only** the missing words **IN CAPITAL LETTERS on a separate answer sheet.**

---

25   One of the footballers was too ill to play that afternoon.

   PREVENTED

   One of the footballers .... by illness that afternoon.

26   I'd prefer you not to eat in the car, if you don't mind.

   WHILE

   I'd rather you .... in the car.

27   I find it amazing that the young singer performs so confidently.

   HOW

   What amazes .... the young singer performs.

28   The price of laptop computers has gone down a lot in recent years.

   FALL

   There has .... price of laptop computers in recent years.

29   The band's pianist finds it fairly easy to learn new songs.

   COMES

   Learning new songs .... the band's pianist.

30   Applicants for the post need to demonstrate that they are both flexible and patient.

   COMBINATION

   Applicants for the post need to demonstrate .... patience.

Part 5

You are going to read an article about a famous designer. For questions **31 – 36**, choose the answer (**A**, **B**, **C** or **D**) which you think fits best according to the text.

In the exam, you mark your answers **on a separate answer sheet**.

The Egg Chair

The Egg Chair, one of the most enduring symbols of the modernist movement in design, was created in a Danish garage over 60 years ago. Today, the quirky futuristic armchair is more extraordinarily popular than ever before. For decades, the unmistakable swivel-seats have brightened up fashionable interiors all over the world, starred in Hollywood blockbusters such as *Men in Black,* and jazzed-up countless trendy hotels, offices, bars and clubs. Genuine Egg Chairs, still made by the Danish company Fritz Hansen and priced at a hefty £5,000, sell by the thousand all over the world. Cheaper reproductions, at anything from £500 to £2,000, have been snapped up by the million. Right now, they've never been more popular and original examples from the 1950s have sold at auction in New York for up to $70,000.

For all this, we must thank one man: Arne Jacobsen, a reclusive architect who rarely left his Copenhagen studio. He designed the Egg Chair as part of a commission to create a new landmark hotel in the centre of the city in the 1950s. The SAS Royal Hotel, which was owned by the airline of the same name, was to be the largest hotel in Denmark, and the first sky-scraper in the country's history. Compared unkindly by critics to a 'glass cigarbox', the rectangular steel structure remains a sort of monument to the modernist movement, and Jacobsen, who is arguably the most important Scandinavian designer of the 20th century, pioneered the modernist movement in which architects began to design both the interiors, and the actual day-to-day contents of their buildings.

"At the SAS hotel, this meant he created everything from the door handles and cutlery to the carpets and colour scheme," says Gemma Curtin, a curator at the Design Museum. "His philosophy was described as 'from spoon to city', and the chair was part of that. The Egg Chair has soft sides. It's really organic, and stems from nature: it looks like a broken shell that a little chick has just run out of. It's sophisticated and minimalist, but still has a sense of fun. You can't imagine a child walking past without wanting to jump in. It's just incredibly warm and relaxing."

Jacobsen built the prototype of the chair in his garage in Copenhagen in 1957. After several minor adjustments, it was unveiled to the public at a local design show. When the hotel opened, Egg Chairs filled the lobby and bar area, and were found in every bedroom. Fritz Hansen, then an up-market, family-owned furniture manufacturer, was handed a contract to build replicas for fashion-conscious homeowners. In keeping with the tradition that true classics develop gradually, the Egg Chair took a while to catch on, and initial sales were disappointing. But by the mid 1960s, buyers had grown to love its revolutionary design.

The design expert Stephen Bayley includes the Egg Chair in *Design: Intelligence Made Visible*, his new guide to modern design classics co-authored by Sir Terence Conran. He believes that "chair design ended" in the late 1950s. "This was when Charles Eames produced his Aluminium Group classics, and Arne Jacobsen his Egg," he says. "Since then, there have been no changes in human physiology, nor the discovery of any relevant new materials, and no genuine improvements in what a modern chair might be. Jacobsen's achievement was to turn the austerity of functionalism into something elegant and spare, yet luxurious as well. He thought of architecture and furniture design as two expressions of the same desire to achieve both physical and psychological comfort."

Antique Egg Chairs can now command a staggering sum. "I've watched this grow and grow since the birth of the modern design auction," says James Zematis, the director of 20th century design at Sotheby's in New York. "There's a surging demand for all post-war Danish furniture." The sky-high prices have led to a burgeoning market in Egg Chair thefts, which Fritz Hansen are attempting to combat by holding a database of serial numbers which all genuine Eggs have carved into the foot. "And you can always tell a fake," says the company's spokesman, Jan Helleskov. "I look at things like the stitching and the dimensions, and the basic shape and the fabric. We've never come across an imitation purporting to be an Egg Chair that we couldn't spot at a glance."

31 Which adjective, used later in the first paragraph, reinforces the idea that the Egg Chair was 'quirky' (line 2)?

- **A** unmistakable
- **B** trendy
- **C** hefty
- **D** sought-after

32 What do we learn about the SAS Royal Hotel in the second paragraph?

- **A** Only parts of it were designed by Arne Jacobsen.
- **B** Not everybody appreciated its design at the time.
- **C** It was made of materials not previously used in Denmark.
- **D** Part of it has since been turned into a museum of architecture.

33 According to Gemma Curtin, the Egg Chair

- **A** was inspired by aspects of the natural world.
- **B** has not always been taken seriously by designers.
- **C** is more practical than many people imagine it will be.
- **D** reflects a philosophy no longer important in modern design.

34 In the fourth paragraph, we learn that when the Egg Chair first went on show,

- **A** it had design faults that were later rectified.
- **B** it was already being mass-produced by a company.
- **C** it did not immediately become a commercial success.
- **D** it was recognised as a design that would become highly influential.

35 According to Stephen Bayley, the Egg Chair

- **A** has adapted well to the use of new materials.
- **B** remains the best design for its intended purpose.
- **C** has tended to prevent new chair designs being appreciated.
- **D** continues to achieve only one of its creator's two main aims.

36 The writer quotes Jan Helleskov in order to show how

- **A** worried the original makers are about fakes.
- **B** the original makers help chair owners to avoid theft.
- **C** well made an original chair from the 1960s actually is.
- **D** easy it is for the company to identify a fake reproduction.

Part 6

You are going to read four reviews of a collection of short stories. For questions **37 – 40**, choose from the critics **A – D**. The critics may be chosen more than once.

In the exam, you mark your answers **on a separate answer sheet**.

Critic A

Nancy Belmont's latest collection of short stories marks an interesting departure from her previous work. Already a successful fiction stylist, Belmont has a parallel career as an acclaimed food writer. These ten short stories are a hybrid of the two activities. Each is set in a different city and is framed around solving a family difficulty over a hearty meal. It sounds enticing, but combining the ingredients proves rather tricky. The various cities are confidently evoked in brief word portraits and the family theme is handled with the sensitivity and insight we've come to expect from Belmont. Sadly, however, the main players in each of the dinner-table dramas which unfold are curiously lacking in empathy, making it hard for the reader to turn to each successive episode with enthusiasm. Reproducing the actual recipes is a brave move – but in reality, who would turn to a book of short stories for tips on lasagne making?

Critic B

The conceit that family differences can and often are resolved over a shared meal is at the heart of Nancy Belmont's new book of short stories. Her protagonists and their human weaknesses are deftly drawn and subtly appealing, and the thread that runs through these stories of effectively sorting out problems over a lengthy dinner at home never palls. You'd think it would be hard to sustain the momentum, but Belmont manages to pull it off. Each meal takes place in a different capital and Belmont's sparkling prose brings each location vividly to life in a few brief sentences – often invoking iconic architectural features to make them instantly recognisable. Choosing to feature step-by-step instructions for making the dishes consumed is a novel and highly entertaining twist – I can personally vouch for the apple pie on page 122.

Critic C

A collection of stories each based in a different city, focusing on the preparation and consumption of food, sounds like something that would keep even the most world-weary traveller entertained and attentive. The actual treatment of cosmopolitan living in Nancy Belmont's new volume is patchy, however. Although she manages to conjure up Beijing so that the reader can almost smell the cloying summer heat, her characters tucking in to a family meal in Paris, could frankly be anywhere. That's not to say that the Parisian family aren't just as likable and engaging as those in the other stories – who are almost without fail amusing and sensitively drawn. Listing ingredients and providing detailed instructions for preparing the dishes themselves is an unexpected and neat device, which works well in reinforcing Belmont's underlying message – that making and sharing food is the key to family relationships the world over.

Critic D

It's a rare book of short stories that has me checking the contents of kitchen cupboards, but readers of Nancy Belmont's latest collection benefit from tips on how to cook the many fine meals her protagonists argue and make peace over. Just as the recipes vary, so do the locations as she takes us on a whistle-stop tour of major cities. The urban settings are international, and so too is the food, to the point where this reader sometimes found it hard to recall in which metropolis the current story was set. Food is prepared, the family gathers, food is consumed. It's a simple formula, and one rich with potential, but it's a challenge to sustain interest over ten stories, even for a writer as skilled as Belmont, who seems more comfortable supplying deft and amusing descriptions of her diners than in pointing us to universal truths about the curative powers of sharing food.

Which critic

shares A's view about the descriptions of the places featured in the stories? 37

has a different opinion to the other three about the inclusion of **a cookery section in the book?** 38

shares B's opinion of how successfully the main theme is handled? 39

has a different opinion to C regarding the appeal of the main **characters in the stories?** 40

Part 7

You are going to read an extract from a wildlife magazine. Six paragraphs have been removed from the article. Choose from the paragraphs **A – G** the one which fits each gap (**41 – 46**). There is one extra paragraph which you do not need to use.

In the exam, you mark your answers **on a separate answer sheet**.

Don't fear the beaver

Cursed with a reputation for destruction, the beaver is now coming to be seen as eco-friendly.

It took years of research and planning, but finally everything was ready. After an absence of at least 200 years, beavers looked set to return to mainland Britain, one of the final frontiers in their reintroduction across Europe. The plan was to release them into a secluded valley in a forest in the west of Scotland and see how they got on. Popular support was strong but last-minute lobbying from powerful local landowners resulted in the Scottish Executive refusing permission. Once again, it seemed, these shy herbivores had fallen foul of their reputation for eco-destruction.

| 41 |

The beaver's love of hydrological engineering has in fact brought it into conflict with people across Europe and North America for centuries, so it's no small irony that experts are now realising that this is exactly why we need beavers in the countryside. "They are the quintessential ecosystem engineers," says ecologist James Byers at the University of New Hampshire. "And they'll do this work for free."

| 42 |

Pursued for centuries by hunters keen to transform their fur into luxury waterproof hats, beavers were probably saved from extinction only by a change of fashion in the 1840s. By the beginning of the 20th century, tiny populations of the European beaver, Castor fiber, survived in just a few rivers in Russia, Norway, France and Germany. Meanwhile, across the Atlantic, the closely related North American species *Castor canadensis* clung on only in Canada's remote boreal forests.

| 43 |

"The reintroduction of the beaver in Europe has been an outstanding success," says Andrew Kitchener, principal curator of mammals and birds at National Museums Scotland in Edinburgh. "Immensely adaptable, they feed on a wide range of herbaceous plants and can set up home in almost any freshwater environment."

| 44 |

In North America this is even more the case than in Europe. But 'proactive management' is encouraging people to learn to live with them there too. One useful tool is the 'beaver deceiver', a perforated plastic pipe that beavers find impossible to plug up. Inserted into an inconvenient dam, beaver deceivers create permanent leaks which keep water levels at a chosen maximum.

| 45 |

Accepting beavers as neighbours is one thing, but many experts now believe we should be actively promoting their spread into their former ranges. For a start, they say, beavers bring ecological benefits by creating ponds upstream of their dams – instant wetlands recreating those destroyed through centuries of drainage campaigns.

| 46 |

It could be a similar story in those places where beavers remain unwelcome. "Beavers would create habitats suitable for up to 32 species in need of urgent conservation action," says Rob Strachan of the UK's Environment Agency. Critics ask why money should be put into bringing back one species? But when lots of other animals and plants benefit too – it makes for extremely cost-effective conservation.

A When they choose large rivers for this, they burrow into the banks and build underwater entrances to their 'lodges', which are invisible to humans. In small waterways, however, they construct dams of mud and timber to raise water levels and create ponds in which they can then recreate the same kind of safe shelter. It is these structures that are perceived as a nuisance.

B Today, both species are steadily re-colonising their original ranges, through a combination of planned releases and natural spread. Now re-established in 26 European countries, beavers are missing from only a handful including mainland Britain (there is no evidence that beavers have ever lived in Ireland).

C These beaver 'ghost towns' are another familiar feature in the wetlands because beavers move along when their preferred food plants are depleted, allowing vegetation to regenerate. In the process they become agents for renewal, helping to create dynamic, biodiverse landscapes.

D In the Adirondack mountains of New York, for instance, the habitats created by beavers along river banks are rich in plants found nowhere else. In Canada, ecologists have discovered that monitoring the still waters behind beaver dams is the best way to study amphibian populations – the frogs and toads can barely survive anywhere else.

E Beaver-built waterworks not only create habitats for wildlife, he explains, they also boost water quality and reduce the twin threats of drought and flooding. In fact, the beaver could even be an invaluable ally in battling the effects of climate change.

F Beavers are no strangers to such opposition. In this case, people feared they would damage valuable salmon stocks in local rivers. Beavers don't eat fish – though plenty of people think they do – but the local groups mistakenly imagined their dams would cause problems. It's an old, misbegotten story.

G Another device, essentially a sturdy wire-mesh cage, prevents beavers blocking culverts and flooding roads. Trees can be protected by wrapping them in wire mesh, or by coating tree trunks with a sand-rich paint. In the future, chemical repellents containing extracts from unpalatable plants may do the job.

Part 8

You are going to read an article about four businesswomen. For questions **47 – 56**, choose from the sections (**A – D**). The sections may be chosen more than once.

In the exam, you mark your answers **on a separate answer sheet**.

Which of the businesswomen

realises how fortunate she was to find an effective way of promoting her products?	47
did some informal market research before starting her business?	48
was at first disappointed by the response to her publicity?	49
had no choice but to find a new career path?	50
felt that her previous career lacked promotion prospects?	51
admits to having no experience whatsoever in the field she entered?	52
produced her own publicity material?	53
says she didn't feel committed to a previous career?	54
got business as a result of word-of-mouth recommendations?	55
waited until she felt confident enough to leave a previous position?	56

New directions

Four businesswomen who risked everything to make their fortune

A Annie Westmorland: recruitment consultancy

I'd worked for years in marketing, and had an MBA degree, yet never seemed to be in the running for a more senior position, which was frustrating. One day, a work contact asked if I knew anyone suitable for a post he was trying to fill. I put some names forward, and one of those people was recruited. That got me thinking about becoming a recruitment consultant. I did a bit of discreet networking, asking some business contacts if they'd use me if I set myself up as one. The response was good, but it still took me a year to summon up the courage to quit my job and go for it. My first job was to find six salespeople for a communications company. I placed an advert in a local business paper and waited. Gradually the CVs came in. I did dozens of interviews and filled all the places. After that, the work rolled in and I'm now well ahead of my projected turnover for the year.

B Zoe Wong: clothing company

I was lying on a beach trying to think of something to wear one evening that I didn't have to iron. That sparked an idea: how fantastic if all my dresses could be wrinkle-free and ready-to-wear. I got very excited and couldn't wait to get home and start researching. I was a complete novice in the fashion world. I was working as a sports-marketing and publicity consultant but my heart wasn't in it. Starting my own business seemed to be the answer to a lot of problems. Using my savings, I got on a plane to Thailand and spent a couple of weeks researching fabrics that looked silky and expensive, yet were almost crease-free. It was scary, but I had faith that the dresses would sell. My lucky break came when a friend managed to get me a cheap advert in an upmarket glossy magazine. She helped me arrange a photo shoot with glamorous models wearing the dresses. It cost a lot, but after that the orders flooded in. You have to be a risk-taker to make a business work, but if you're successful, the rewards are huge.

C Melanie Hardisty: event-planning business

The idea came when I was asked to arrange a social event for members of the gym I went to. It occurred to me that this was a service that you could sell to companies, and something I could do without huge amounts of experience. I had no idea if it would work. My first event was a golf day with a gourmet meal in the evening. I went for a date six weeks ahead and booked everything up, but set aside part of my life savings to cover my costs if it was a disaster. I made up some flyers on my computer, then spent a weekend in town handing them out and texting everyone I knew. Initially there wasn't much interest and I thought I'd made a terrible mistake. But then the phone started ringing and the event was soon fully-booked. The day was a great success and I made a profit.

D Fiorella Lucchesi: web-design business

I started up through necessity – I was made redundant from my accountancy job, and couldn't get another. I thought I'd brush up on my computer skills and did a course. But I wasted my money because it wasn't up to much. Not to be discouraged, I bought lots of books and taught myself. I'd always been interested in website design and thought it was an area where I could make some money. A friend saw some designs I'd done and mentioned my name to someone who wanted a website for his hypnotherapy business. I'd no idea what to charge, so I said the first number that came into my head, which was £700, and he agreed. It only took me a couple of days and he was delighted with the results. Word spread among the alternative therapy community and I got more work than I could cope with. I only needed to design two websites a week to make the salary I'd been earning before. In my first month I designed four websites and in the second month I did six.

Part 1

You must answer this question. Write your answer in **220 – 260** words in an appropriate style.

In the exam, you write your answer **on a separate answer sheet**.

---

1   In your class you have listened to a radio discussion about the importance of the arts in modern society, and whether theatres and art galleries are still needed. You have made the notes below:

> **How important are the arts in modern society?**
> - need for escapism
> - appreciating beauty
> - cost of funding
>
> Some opinions expressed in the discussion:
>
> "We don't need theatres because we can see films and television programmes which have better effects."
>
> "Art is for all time and everyone should be able to see it."
>
> "It's expensive to maintain art galleries and the money could be spent on sports facilities."

Write an essay discussing **two** of the ideas in your notes about the importance of the arts. You should **explain which one is most important**, **giving reasons** to support your opinion.

You may, if you wish, make use of the opinions expressed in the discussion, but you should use your own words as far as possible.

Part 2

Write an answer to **one** of the questions **2 – 4** in this part. Write your answer in **220 – 260** words in an appropriate style. In the exam, you write your answer **on a separate answer sheet,** and put the question number in the box at the top of the page.

---

2   A new cinema complex has just opened in your town, and the local newspaper wants people to write reviews of the centre.

Write a review for the newspaper saying what's in the complex, how you felt about it, whether there is anything you would like to see done to improve it and whether you would recommend seeing films there.

Write your **review**.

3   You have received this email from an English friend:

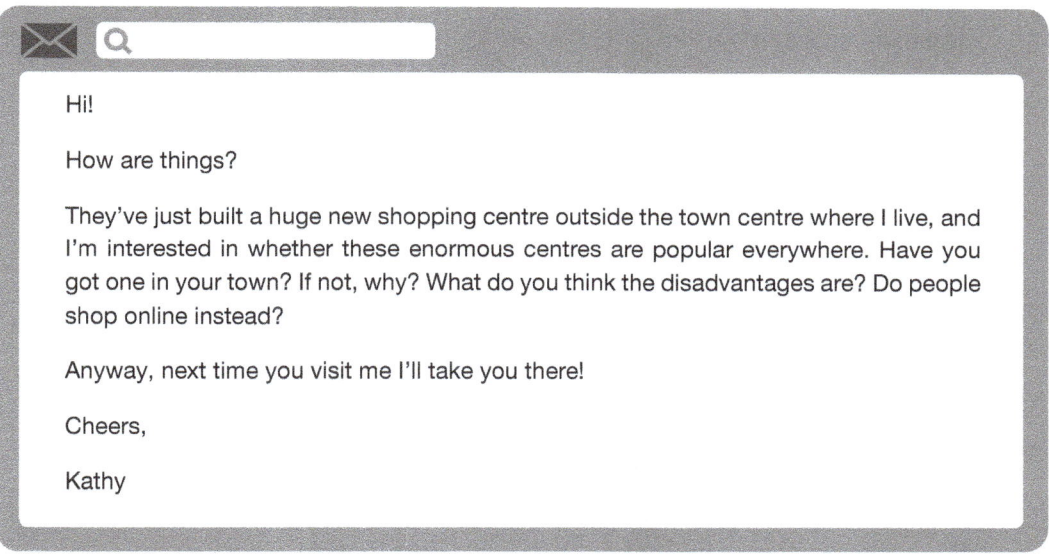

Hi!

How are things?

They've just built a huge new shopping centre outside the town centre where I live, and I'm interested in whether these enormous centres are popular everywhere. Have you got one in your town? If not, why? What do you think the disadvantages are? Do people shop online instead?

Anyway, next time you visit me I'll take you there!

Cheers,

Kathy

Write your **email**.

4   You have just finished a short period of work experience in the office of a local company. Now the company has asked you to write a report on your experience.

Your report should explain how successful you feel your time with the company was, describe any problems you had and suggest any ways in which the company could improve the experience for other people.

Write your **report**.

Part 1

You will hear three different extracts. For questions **1 – 6**, choose the answer (**A, B** or **C**) which fits best according to what you hear. There are two questions for each extract.

In the exam, you write your answers on **a separate answer sheet**.

Extract One

You overhear two friends discussing a film they have seen recently.

1. What do they agree about the film?

    A The storyline was weak.
    B The overall message was unclear.
    C There was too little historical detail.

2. The man feels that the film

    A must have been better in the original language.
    B should not have been billed as a comedy.
    C can't have cost much to make.

Extract Two

You hear part of a documentary about a businessman called Matt Ticknall.

3. What does the presenter suggest about Matt's honeymoon?

    A It was foolish of him to go ahead with the trip.
    B It was unfair of him to keep bad news from his wife.
    C It was kind of him to keep his business problems to himself.

4. Matt says that at the time of his wedding,

    A he was confident that his business would improve.
    B he had mistimed the development of a new product.
    C he couldn't understand how he lost so much money.

Extract Three

You hear part of a discussion about the pace of modern life.

5   The woman feels that the article she's read is

   A   exaggerated.
   B   highly original.
   C   thought-provoking.

6   What point was made on the TV programme the man saw?

   A   People need to develop their free-time activities.
   B   Attitudes towards leisure time have changed over the years.
   C   Social problems can result from having too much spare time.

Part 2

You will hear part of a programme about a man called Lewis Pugh who plans to swim the entire length of the River Thames. For questions **7 – 14**, complete the sentences with a word or short phrase.

In the exam, you mark your answers **on a separate answer sheet**.

Lewis Pugh: long-distance swimmer

Lewis generally swims without the protection of either body oil or a

(7) ....

The subject which Lewis studied at university was (8) ....

There is a (9) ....

to show where the source of the River Thames is.

It will take Lewis (10) .... to swim the entire length of the river.

Lewis will start swimming early each morning to avoid being affected by

(11) ....

On the tidal section of the river, coming into contact with

(12) .... is the greatest hazard.

In London, Lewis has invited journalists and scientists to an outdoor

(13) ....

To raise money for his swims, Lewis does what he calls

(14) ....

Part 3

You will hear an interview with Hilary Bradt, who is the author and publisher of a series of guidebooks. For questions **15 – 20**, choose the answer (**A, B, C** or **D**) which fits best according to what you hear.

In the exam, write your answers **on a separate answer sheet**.

---

15 When asked about her earliest travel memories, Hilary suggests that

  A she still needs help to find her way.
  B she really prefers to explore new places alone.
  C her mother instilled a love of adventure in her.
  D her main reason for travelling is to meet new people.

16 What made Hilary decide to make a career of travel writing?

  A her frustration at the lack of guidebooks for adventurous travellers
  B the realisation that it was possible to publish your own work
  C a need to find a way of financing future hiking expeditions
  D a chance meeting with someone willing to publish her work

17 What plans does Hilary have for the immediate future?

  A She's hoping to train as a teacher.
  B She intends to take up a new hobby.
  C She wants to update one of her books.
  D She's looking forward to doing more writing.

18 When talking about her charity work in Madagascar, Hilary asks listeners to

  A consider joining a visit to a children's centre.
  B assist with the making of items of clothing.
  C help her to transport things to the country.
  D make a donation to a children's project.

19 Hilary says that she's irritated by travellers who reveal

  A a lack of respect for local trading customs.
  B a reluctance to support the local economy.
  C an unwillingness to pay the full price for goods.
  D an assumption that local traders will try to cheat them.

20 For Hilary, the best sort of travellers

  A have a broad-minded attitude towards local cultures.
  B research a country thoroughly before visiting it.
  C are willing to use a variety of transport options.
  D try to avoid changing the lives of local people.

Part 4

You will hear five short extracts in which people are talking about their work.

In the exam, mark your answers **on a separate answer sheet.**

TASK ONE

For questions **21 – 25**, choose from the list (**A – H**) the sector each speaker works in.

TASK TWO

For questions **26 – 30**, choose from the list (**A – H**) what each person is doing as they speak.

While you listen you must complete both tasks.

A   agriculture
B   e-commerce
C   education
D   fashion
E   fine art
F   law
G   medicine
H   security

21	Speaker 1
22	Speaker 2
23	Speaker 3
24	Speaker 4
25	Speaker 5

A   complaining about the attitude of others
B   suggesting how problems can be avoided
C   emphasising the thoroughness of a process
D   explaining how a selection is made
E   describing how an idea developed
F   justifying an important change of direction
G   outlining a range of responsibilities
H   regretting the rigidity of a system

26	Speaker 1
27	Speaker 2
28	Speaker 3
29	Speaker 4
30	Speaker 5

Part 1 (2 minutes)

The examiner will ask you one or two questions about yourself and what you think about everyday topics such as work or study, travel, holidays, daily life and routines.

- Do you often use social media? (Why / Why not?)
- How do you usually keep up with the news? (Why?)
- Is there a new skill you'd really like to learn one day? (Why / Why not?)

Part 2 (4 minutes)

Turn to the pictures on page 188, which show **people taking a short break**.

TAKING A BREAK

Candidate A, I'd like you to compare two of the pictures, and say **why the people might need to take a short break, and how they might feel if they didn't do this**.

Candidate B, **who do you think needs the short break the most? (Why?)**

DOING THINGS CAREFULLY

Turn to the pictures on page 190, which show people doing things carefully.

Candidate B, compare two of the pictures and say **why it might be important for the people to do these things carefully and what might happen if they don't take great care**.

Candidate A, **who do you think needs to do the things most carefully? (Why?)**

Part 3 (4 minutes)

Turn to the task on page 189, which shows things governments often choose to spend public money on.

Now, talk to each other about **how important it is for governments to spend public money on these things**.

Now decide **which one governments should spend most public money on**.

Part 4 (5 minutes)

Answer these questions.

- Who do you think should regulate the way governments spend money? (Why?)
- Which do you think is more important for governments to support financially – science, or the arts? (Why?)
- Should governments do more to protect the environment? (Why / Why not?)
- Some governments spend money on awareness raising campaigns for things like environmental issues. Is this a good idea? (Why / Why not?)
- Is it important for governments to fund elite athletes who are training for international competitions? (Why / Why not?)
- If you could advise governments, what sort of things would you like them to spend money on? (Why?)

SPEAKING **TEST 7**

GENERAL MARK SCHEME FOR SPEAKING

Assessment scales

Throughout the test, candidates are assessed on their own individual performance and not in relation to each other. They are awarded marks by two examiners: the assessor and the interlocutor. The assessor awards marks by applying performance descriptors from the analytical assessment scales for the following criteria:

- Grammatical resource
- Lexical resource
- Discourse management
- Pronunciation
- Interactive communication

The interlocutor awards a mark for Global Achievement using the Global Achievement scale. Assessment for *Cambridge English: Advanced* is based on performance across all parts of the test, and is achieved by applying the relevant descriptors in the assessment scales.

Grammatical resource

This refers to the accurate and appropriate use of a range of both simple and complex grammatical forms. Performance is viewed in terms of the overall effectiveness of the language used in spoken interaction.

Lexical resource

This refers to the candidate's ability to use a range of vocabulary to meet task requirements. At the Advanced level, the tasks require candidates to speculate and exchange views on unfamiliar topics. Performance is viewed in terms of the overall effectiveness of the language used in spoken interaction.

Discourse management

This refers to the candidate's ability to link extended utterances together to form coherent speech, without undue hesitation. The utterances should be relevant to the tasks and should be arranged clearly and logically to develop the themes or arguments required by the tasks.

Pronunciation

This refers to the candidate's ability to produce intelligent utterances to fulfil the task requirements. This includes stress and intonation, as well as individual sounds. Examiners put themselves in the position of a non-ESOL specialist and assess the overall impact of the pronunciation on the listener and the degree of effort required to understand the candidate.

Interactive communication

This refers to the candidate's ability to take an active part in the development of the discourse. This requires an ability to participate in the range of interactive situations in the rest, and to develop discussions on a range of topics by initiating and responding appropriately. This also refers to the deployment of strategies to maintain interaction at an appropriate level throughout the test so that the tasks can be fulfilled.

Global achievement

This refers to the candidate's overall effectiveness in dealing with the tasks in the four separate parts of the Advanced Speaking test. The global mark is an independent impression mark which reflects the assessment of the candidate's performance from the interlocutor's perspective.

SPEAKING BANK

Part 1

In Part 1, you answer individual questions from the interlocutor on personal topics such as your likes and dislikes, everyday life and routines, work, holiday preferences and so on. This takes about two minutes.

Watch the full test online.

Exam help

- ✓ Only answer your own questions. Don't contribute to your partner's answers.
- ✓ Give answers that are interesting, but not too long.
- ✓ Don't just answer yes or no – always give a reason for your answer.
- ✓ This part of the test should put you at your ease. Imagine you're in a social situation and meeting someone for the first time. Think about how you might answer general social questions such as the following.
  - What kind of television programmes do you enjoy? Why?
  - What kind of magazines or newspapers do you read regularly? Why?
  - Do you ever listen to the radio? Why / Why not?
  - What time of day do you find best for studying? Why?
  - What do you like to do when you go out with your friends? Why?
  - Do you have a particularly busy life generally? Why / Why not?
  - Do you think it's useful to have a daily routine? Why / Why not?

Useful language

Responding to questions

I really enjoy … because …
I'm afraid I don't really like … because …
I rarely … because …
My family consists of …
My favourite … is … as …
I choose to … whenever I can. That suits me best.
In the future, I'd really like to …, since …
I think my friends might say …, but in my personal opinion …
I don't know what to say – it's a difficult question, but probably …
I don't think I really have a preference, although if I had to choose I'd say …
I haven't thought about that before! It's an interesting question …

Part 2

In Part 2, you compare two pictures from a choice of three, and say something else about them. You have to speak for about a minute. After you've spoken, your partner will be asked a short question on the topic of your pictures.

Watch the full test online.

Exam help

- Listen carefully to the interlocutor's instructions, and only ask for them to be repeated if you really didn't understand. If the interlocutor repeats the task, you'll lose time from your minute.
- The questions are written above the pictures to help you. Remember to compare the two pictures you choose before you answer these questions. The questions give you the chance to speculate and show a range of language.
- Spend about 20 seconds comparing the pictures, and the remaining time dealing with the rest of the task. This will help you to manage your time and organise your ideas coherently.
- Only compare two of the pictures, otherwise you will run out of time.
- Don't describe what you can see in the pictures – you should compare and speculate. Don't read the questions out loud before you start, as you will lose time.

Useful language

Comparing the pictures
Both pictures seem to be about …
Whereas the people in the first picture are busy, those in the second picture are …
The first picture shows a workplace. Conversely, the second …
Clearly, the people in the second picture are enjoying themselves more than …
There's a big difference in how the people are feeling …

Expressing opinions
It seems obvious to me that …
What I think is …
It seems quite clear that …
I feel quite strongly that …
In my view …

Speculating
I'm not totally certain, but …
I'd probably say that …
I'm not really sure; it's just a guess, but …
They could well be …
Perhaps they're feeling … because …
It looks as though …
They could be … because …

Organising your talk
I'll start by comparing …
In the first place …
Both pictures show ….
To add to what I said about …
On top of that, I'd say …
Against that idea is the fact that …
On the other hand …

Part 3

In Part 3, you discuss a task with your partner. You're given a question with five written prompts to talk about. You have to discuss these prompts in as much detail as you can, and respond appropriately to what your partner says. After two minutes the interlocutor stops you and gives you another related question to discuss and reach a decision.

Watch the full test online.

Exam help

- Try to say as much as you can about each prompt before moving on to the next. Don't worry if you can't talk about all of the prompts in the time – it's more important to have a detailed discussion.
- Make sure you and your partner take it in turns to initiate your discussion.
- It's important that you listen to each other. Respond to what your partner has said before moving the discussion on to the next prompt.
- When you're asked to make a decision, use the whole minute to discuss your ideas. Don't make a decision too quickly. It doesn't matter if you can't decide – the important thing is the language you use.

Useful language

Agreeing/disagreeing
You made a good point when you said …
I take your point. Absolutely …
I'm with you on that …
I'm not sure. Don't you think that …
I guess that's true, but obviously …
You said … , but I'm afraid I can't agree …
I don't see how that's relevant …
I can't see what you're getting at …

Justifying and clarifying
So when you said … you meant …
What I intended to say was …
The reason I say this is …
So what you really mean is …
I actually meant that …

Initiating and moving on to another prompt
I'm not sure what to say about this one. What do you think?
What does this add?
We haven't thought about this one yet.
How about considering this one …?
I think this is similar to … . In fact, we could link the ideas together.

Asking for opinions
How do you feel about …?
Are you with me on that one?
Do you feel the same?
Is there anything you'd like to add …?

Summarising for the decision question
So we seem to be saying that the most difficult skill would be …
Taking into consideration everything you've mentioned I think we're agreed that …
So, on balance we think …

SPEAKING BANK

Part 4

In Part 4, you discuss abstract questions related to the topic you discussed in Part 3. You should give more detailed answers than you did in Part 1, and you can discuss the questions with your partner if you like.

Watch the full test online.

Exam help

- The interlocutor may ask one of you a direct question, or ask a question to both of you. Even if the interlocutor asks your partner a question, you can still add your own ideas once your partner has answered. You don't have to agree with your partner.
- If you're not sure of the answer to your own question, or have no ideas, use fillers to gain time to think, or ask your partner for their opinion.
- There are no 'right' answers to these questions – you simply have to express your opinions. The questions give you the chance to show your range of language.

Useful language

Using 'fillers' to gain time to think
Let me consider that …
That's a good question! Just a minute … Ah yes, what I think is …
Hmm … let's see …
Give me a moment …
I've never thought about it before, but what I'd say is …
I'm not really sure what to say. Do you have any ideas?

Responding to a question
What I think about that is …
It seems to me that …
This question is really interesting/difficult because …
I've actually thought about this before, and I feel that …
Great question! It's tricky though, because …

Developing an answer
So if I really think about it, I could add that …
It also occurs to me that …
What I said before doesn't mean that …
To add to what I've already said …
To go into it a bit further, I'd say that …
The reason I think this is …
What I'm saying is … because …
To explain more about what I mean …
For instance, when I was …

Adding to your partner's answer
I agree with … , and can I just add that …
She said … and that's a good example to use.
To clarify my views on what she said, …
I think she's absolutely right, and on top of that …

SPEAKING BANK

GENERAL MARK SCHEME FOR WRITING

Band 5
For a Band 5 to be awarded, the candidate's writing has a very positive effect on the target reader. The content is relevant* and the topic is fully developed. Information and ideas are skilfully organised through a range of cohesive devices, which are used to good effect. A wide range of complex structures and vocabulary is used effectively. Errors are minimal, and inaccuracies which do occur have no impact on communication. Register and format are consistently appropriate to the purpose of the task and the audience.

Band 4
For a Band 4 to be awarded, the candidate's writing has a positive effect on the target reader. The content is relevant* and the topic is developed. Information and ideas are clearly organised through the use of a variety of cohesive devices. A good range of complex structures and vocabulary is used. Some errors may occur with vocabulary and when complex language is attempted, but these do not cause difficulty for the reader. Register and format are usually appropriate to the purpose of the task and the audience.

Band 3
For a Band 3 to be awarded, the candidate's writing has a satisfactory effect on the target reader. The content is relevant* with some development of the topic. Information and ideas are generally organised logically, though cohesive devices may not always be used appropriately. A satisfactory range of structures and vocabulary is used, though word choice may lack precision. Errors which do occur do not cause difficulty for the reader. Register and format are reasonably appropriate to the purpose of the task and the audience.

Band 2
For a Band 2 to be awarded, the candidate's writing has a negative effect on the target reader. The content is not always relevant. Information and ideas are inadequately organised and sometimes incoherent, with inaccurate use of cohesive devices. The range of structures and vocabulary is limited and/or repetitive, and errors may be basic or cause difficulty for the reader. Register and format are sometimes inappropriate to the purpose of the task and the audience.

Band 1
For a Band 1 to be awarded, the candidate's writing has a very negative effect on the target reader. The content is often irrelevant. Information and ideas are poorly organised, often incoherent, and there is minimal use of cohesive devices. The range of structures and vocabulary is severely limited, and errors frequently cause considerable difficulty for the reader. Register and format are inappropriate to the purpose of the task and the audience.

Band 0
For a Band 0 to be awarded, there is either too little language for assessment or the candidate's writing is totally irrelevant or illegible.

* Candidates who do not address all the content points will be penalised for dealing inadequately with the requirements of the task.

Candidates who fully satisfy the Band 3 descriptor will demonstrate an adequate performance in writing at Advanced level.

Part 1 Essay

Exam question

In class you have been discussing why many students have part-time jobs while they are at college. You have made the notes below:

Why college students have part-time jobs
- money
- time
- experience

Some opinions expressed in the discussion:

"Money's great but it isn't everything."

"I'm so tired when I work and study – nothing gets done well."

"It'll stand me in good stead when I'm looking for a real job."

Write an essay discussing **two** of the reasons in your notes. You should **explain which reason is more influential** for college students who choose to have part-time jobs, **giving reasons** to support your answer.

You may, if you wish, make use of the opinions expressed in the discussion, but you should use your own words as far as possible.

Write your answer in **220 – 260** words in an appropriate style.

Exam help

- Read the task carefully. Make sure you have enough ideas about the topic to write 220 – 260 words. The purpose of an essay is to present an argument clearly and coherently, and to provide relevant evidence to support your point of view.
- Choose the two points from the task that you want to discuss, then plan your essay in paragraphs. It's easy to organise your essay if each middle paragraph focuses on one of the two points you have chosen from the task.
- You're presenting an argument with reasons for your opinions, so you must explain your ideas clearly and then justify them. Plan what you want to say, making sure that you've included evidence to support your point of view.
- Remember you can use the opinions given in the task to support your ideas, but don't quote them – you must rewrite them in your own words.
- Use a formal or semi-formal style. It may be appropriate to use rhetorical questions to lead into your argument or introduce your ideas.
- Use a range of vocabulary and structures. You should use language at C1 level.

Essay
- An essay may be written as a result of a class activity such as listening to a radio discussion, having a debate or watching a film. It's usually written for a class tutor, using a formal or semi-formal style.
- The purpose of an essay is to present an argument that will convince the reader of your point of view. It should highlight and discuss important points or issues on a given topic, supporting and developing the argument with extra details which are clarified through reasons and examples.
- Don't begin your essay by explaining what you think. The reader should understand your opinion through the way you present your argument. This means you should finish with a conclusion that summarises your own point of view, and this should be a logical outcome of the argument you've presented. Your conclusion should not come as a surprise.
- Try not to repeat ideas, which can be confusing for the reader. Make your essay a clearly presented, well-developed and logical argument. Each idea should be linked with connectors, and your whole argument should be coherent.
- Although you are arguing towards your conclusion, you should also try to include a balanced discussion of ideas, showing you are aware of all the possible issues, even though you favour one or the other.

Useful language

Introduction
It's often said that …
Many people today think …
This is a hotly-debated subject …
It could be said that …
It's generally accepted that …
This is a topic that is becoming increasingly important …
It is common knowledge that …

Linking ideas
While I can see some benefits, these may be outweighed by the drawbacks …
On the other hand, some students feel that …
In contrast to this point of view …
Although this might seem to be sensible, it could also be …
Conversely, it may be inappropriate for this situation.
On the contrary, it could be the perfect solution to …
Since this is a common issue for students …
Whereas it may seem to be the solution, there are other things to consider …

Giving opinions
For this reason, I …
It seems to me that …
In my opinion, this is due to …
From my perspective, this seems to be …
To be honest, my standpoint is …
Actually, this appears to be overstating the case.
In fact, I feel that …
I strongly believe that …

Conclusion
To sum up the various issues involved, …
On balance I feel that …
In summary, …
In brief …
On the whole, it's clear that …
Overall, the main reason is …
Taking all the arguments into account, I would say that …

Sample answer

There are many reasons why students choose to have part-time jobs while they're still at college, but what really influences them? It may seem an easy answer, but the truth may be more complicated, and it's a topic that is becoming increasingly important.

Firstly, money has to be high on the list. Who doesn't want to earn money? However, working too many hours could have adverse effects on a student's studying habits, as working could distract them from their course and cause their concentration to lapse. Obviously everyone needs money to live, but compromises may have to be made between becoming financially stable and gaining a good qualification.

On the other hand, some students feel that gaining work experience is going to be advantageous when they enter the workplace for real. The old argument about which is more important, qualifications or experience, is relevant here. A student who finishes their course with both a good degree and useful and relevant work experience is going to be in a good position. However, the crucial thing is that the part-time job students choose to do should be relevant to their career plans, and not simply an easy option. So, many choose easy employment such as working as waiters, influenced by the prospect of tips and potential wages.

To sum up the issues involved, it seems to me that these two influences have to be balanced. The desire for money clearly has the greatest influence on college students, but it has disadvantages. Students who see the bigger picture can achieve this balance.

Introduce the topic in general terms, using a rhetorical question to lead in to the discussion.

Insert suitable connectors to link points and paragraphs.

Support your ideas with examples and supporting details.

Use clear paragraphs for each discussion point or issue.

Show that you appreciate other points of view, as this strengthens your argument.

Don't give your own opinion until the final paragraph. Your conclusion should follow your argument clearly.

Part 2 Proposal

Exam question

Your college wants to run a special event to provide advice and information about career and further education opportunities for students. The principal has asked students for proposals for the event outlining what should be included, suggesting how it should be organised and giving reasons for their recommendations.

Write your **proposal**. Write your answer in **220 – 260** words in an appropriate style.

Sample answer

Headings make the proposal easy to read.

The style is formal because it's a proposal. Your introduction should state the purpose of the proposal as it helps you to organise your ideas.

Briefly explain why the proposed recommendations are required.

Explain why your recommendations would be effective.

Use bullet points for clarity, but don't make your language too simple – it should be at an Advanced level.

Include an appropriate conclusion.

Introduction
It is crucial that students receive advice and information about possible careers before leaving college. The purpose of this proposal is to evaluate how a special event could fulfil these needs, and make suggestions and recommendations for how it could be organised.

Background information
Currently there is little practical help available. There is a section in the college library with leaflets from employers and universities, but not much real guidance. A special event would be helpful.

Suggestions and recommendations for an event
- The event should take place over a weekend.
- There should be separate stalls where experts can advise about possible careers and university courses. There could be a video link to different universities. This would be more effective than simply reading leaflets.
- In addition, it would be useful to invite speakers from local companies. They could offer short periods of work experience, which would allow students to try different kinds of work to see what would suit them.
- It would be a good idea to allocate time when a tutor could be on hand to discuss individual requirements. This could be done through an appointments system. The advantage of this is that students would receive personal academic advice.
- I would strongly recommend that the college invite old students to return to describe their own experiences. There is no doubt that young people listen to their peers.
- Finally, there should be workshops on writing a good CV and interview techniques. These skills are invaluable, and rarely taught.

Conclusion
If these recommendations were implemented, the weekend event would be extremely beneficial.

Useful language

Providing background information
The purpose of this proposal is …
One of our priorities is …
One key aspect of our plans …
The current situation is unsatisfactory because …

Making recommendations
It would be a good idea to …
One suggestion would be to …
I would strongly recommend …
It would be possible/useful to …

Giving reasons/supporting recommendations
There is no doubt that …
The advantage is that …
It will give the opportunity to …
There is no better way to …
It would improve …
It is essential/critical that …
There is an urgent need for …

Conclusion
In the light of …
If these recommendations were to be implemented …
It is time to change/add …

Exam help

- ✓ The purpose of a proposal is to give information, not to engage the reader, so techniques like rhetorical questions aren't appropriate.
- ✓ A proposal usually contains suggestions for the future, using modal verbs.
- ✓ Use headings for each section to present information clearly.
- ✓ Bullet points are useful for recommendations. Don't include too many, though. You need to show a range of Advanced language.
- ✓ Support recommendations with evidence using a formal or semi-formal style.

Part 2 Review

Useful language

Using interesting language
It's totally amazing/spectacular …
It has the power to thrill …
It sent a shiver down my spine …
The music is instantly recognisable.

Talking directly to the reader
I'm sure you'll all agree that …
Why not give it a go? You'll find …

Making recommendations
I would certainly recommend …
You should definitely see this!
You'd be mad to miss this …
This is a must-see …

Exam help

- A review is often of a book or a film, but it could also be about an exhibition, an event, a website, etc.
- Plan carefully. Remember that the focus of a review is usually to interest and inform the reader.
- Each paragraph should focus on a different aspect of the review.
- Try to engage the reader by using techniques such as rhetorical questions, although you shouldn't overuse these. Talk directly to the reader.
- The style of a review depends on the context. It may be semi-formal or informal, but you should always use a range of language. Use modifiers and adjectives to help your reader understand your experience.
- Add examples to support your opinions.
- Try to finish in an interesting way. You may have to include a recommendation, even if it is a negative one. Give your own opinion at the end.

Exam question

An international book magazine has asked readers to send in reviews of books they think would be good to read on a long journey. Write a review of a book you feel would be especially good for a long journey, saying what you enjoyed about it and why you would recommend it to other travellers.

Write your review. Write your answer in **220 – 260** words in an appropriate style.

Sample answer

I frequently travel on long journeys, and I know that they are tedious. Some people watch films, but for me a good book is more absorbing and makes the time go faster. So which book would I recommend? ◄ *This engages the reader from the start.*

I've tried different genres, including lengthy classical novels, but in the end I always come back to thrillers. Who doesn't want to solve a mystery? A book like *The Girl on the Train* has all the elements that keep you turning the page. First, although there is a narrator you are not sure whether to trust her. Is she telling you the truth, or is she hiding something? The central character is a mystery in herself, and you are not sure whether you like her or not. Then there is a possible murder, which may or may not have taken place. All these devices are intriguing. ◄ *Don't give away too much information about the plot – just enough to give the reader a flavour of it without spoiling it.*

Add to that the quality of the writing, and you have a real page-turner. The writer uses language very effectively to keep you on your toes – what appears to be described as fact may turn out to be untrue. ◄ *Use interesting and dramatic language.*

The novel is long enough to fill many hours on a journey, and as well as being gripping it is also easy to read. This means there are no demands made on your powers of concentration, so you could doze off if you wanted to – though I doubt that!

For these reasons, I recommend this book for any traveller who wants to become totally absorbed in another world – you may be surprised when you arrive at your destination! ◄ *Finish with a joke or a punchline to reinforce your opinion – remember you want other people to read the book.*

Part 2 Letter

Exam question

You have seen this advert in a travel magazine:

> *Looking for adventure?*
>
> We need four people to take part in a television documentary called *Survival*. You'll live in a remote mountain area for three months with only your teammates for support. You'll keep a video diary of your experiences.
>
> If you think you have the skills to live in a hostile environment and be a useful member of a team, write us a letter explaining why you should be included in the project.

Sample answer

Write your **letter**. Write your answer in **220 – 260** words in an appropriate style.

State your reason for writing at the beginning. This is a formal letter, so use a formal style.

Dear Sir,

I'm writing in response to your announcement calling for participants in the television documentary *Survival*, and I would like to be considered for the role.

Give some background personal information so that the reader will be interested in finding out about you.

Firstly, I'd like you to know a little about me. I'm 22 years old, have a background in extreme sports and am a keen hiker. I am currently working for a climbing equipment company, so I have a good understanding of what is required for challenging environments.

I have been fascinated by the outdoor life since I was young, when my parents took me on camping weekends in the mountains. On these trips I learned how to stay safe in difficult conditions, and to read changes in the weather. Since then I have been on many such trips alone and with friends, and I am extremely self-sufficient. These experiences would stand me in good stead in the environment you describe for your project.

Give examples to support your application.

Although I am very independent, I am also a supportive team player. On one of my mountain trips, a friend fell and broke his leg. It was my responsibility to get him to safety, and to organise rescue. I have a good sense of humour, and get on well with others.

Use connectors so that your letter is easy to follow.

You've been asked to explain why you should be included in the project, so summarise your position at the end.

In addition, I am a good cook and have excellent general survival skills, including first aid. I have always written blogs of my own expeditions, and would relish the task of keeping a video diary for the programme.

For the above reasons, I feel I would be a good candidate for your project, and am very keen to participate.

I look forward to hearing from you.

Finish with an appropriate phrase – in this case it's a formal letter and you don't know the name of the person you are writing to.

Yours faithfully,

Josie

Useful language

Beginning/ending a formal letter/email

Regarding your letter/article …
I am writing in response to …
With reference to your …
I am writing to apply for …
I look forward to hearing from you.
Yours sincerely/faithfully
Best regards/wishes

Beginning/ending an informal letter/email

Thanks so much for …
Sorry not to have written earlier …
I thought it was time I …
It was great to hear from you …
I thought I'd let you know …
Sorry it's taken me so long to …
That's all for now – write back soon!
All the best/Cheers

Referring to a previous letter

With reference to your letter …
You said that you were …
You mentioned …
You asked me to …

Providing information

Firstly, I'd like you to know …
As a teenager, I feel that …
In addition, …

Exam help

- Make sure you understand the purpose of your letter.
- Think carefully about who you're writing to, and how well you know them. Use an appropriate tone.
- If you have to respond to a letter, underline the key points in what they've written so that you include everything they've asked.
- Organise it into clear paragraphs. Use appropriate opening and closing phrases, and give a reason for writing.

Part 2 Report

Useful language

Starting the report
The aim of this report is to …
In this report I will …
This report presents …
This report is intended to …

Giving background information
There are several issues to resolve.
On the course there were disadvantages as well as benefits.

Making recommendations
In the light of … , it seems that the best approach to take would be …
I would recommend … as …
My recommendation would be …
One suggestion would be to …

Finishing the report
For the reasons stated, I feel that …
If these changes were introduced …
In short, I feel confident in recommending …
It seems advisable to …
The above recommendations would be easy to implement …

Exam help

- Read the task carefully to identify the reader and what style to use.
- The purpose of a report is to inform the reader about an existing situation in order for them to make some kind of decision. You should make recommendations and give your own opinion. You need to include appropriate details to support your ideas and suggestions.
- Consider the best layout to use – you can use headings and bullet points, but don't use language that is too simple.
- The format and style should be appropriate for the context.
- Include a conclusion, perhaps with a final evaluation supporting your ideas.

Exam question

Your college wants to help new students settle in to college life easily. The principal has asked the social committee to write a report outlining what is currently done to help new students, identifying things that need improving and making recommendations for how these improvements could be implemented.

Write your **report**. Write your answer in **220 – 260** words in an appropriate style.

Sample answer

Introduction
The aim of this report is to outline the current situation for new students in the college, identify areas that need improving and make recommendations for implementing these improvements.

You can use headings for clarity.

State the aim of the report at the start, and identify what you will do in the report.

Background information
When new students arrive in college they are given an academic orientation programme. However, they are not given any help to integrate into the social life of the college; so many feel isolated and are unsure about how to go about making new friends. This needs improving.

In addition, although there are social and sports clubs, these are not well-advertised and so many new students are unaware of them.

Identify the things that need improving before you make recommendations.

Use connectors to link your ideas.

Recommendations
- There should be a 'buddy' system set up, where existing students would be paired with new students for the first week. This would be enormously beneficial to both parties, as the new student would feel secure and the existing student would gain a new friend.
- In order to integrate new students, there should be a large social gathering across the college at the end of the first week. This could take place in the main hall, and should be organised by the social committee. It would go a long way to putting new students at ease.
- I suggest that a day be set aside for a 'clubs fair' where the social and sports clubs run stalls explaining what they offer and how new students can join. The best time for this would be a day in the second week.

If you use bullet points, vary the way each bullet point is expressed. This will enable you to use a range of advanced language.

Give a reason why your recommendation would be useful.

Conclusion
The above recommendations would be easy to implement, but would greatly improve the experience of new students in the college.

Finish with a conclusion reinforcing your opinion.

VISUALS BANK

Part 2 Candidate A

- Why might the people want to stretch in these situations?
- How important might it be for them to stretch properly?

Part 3

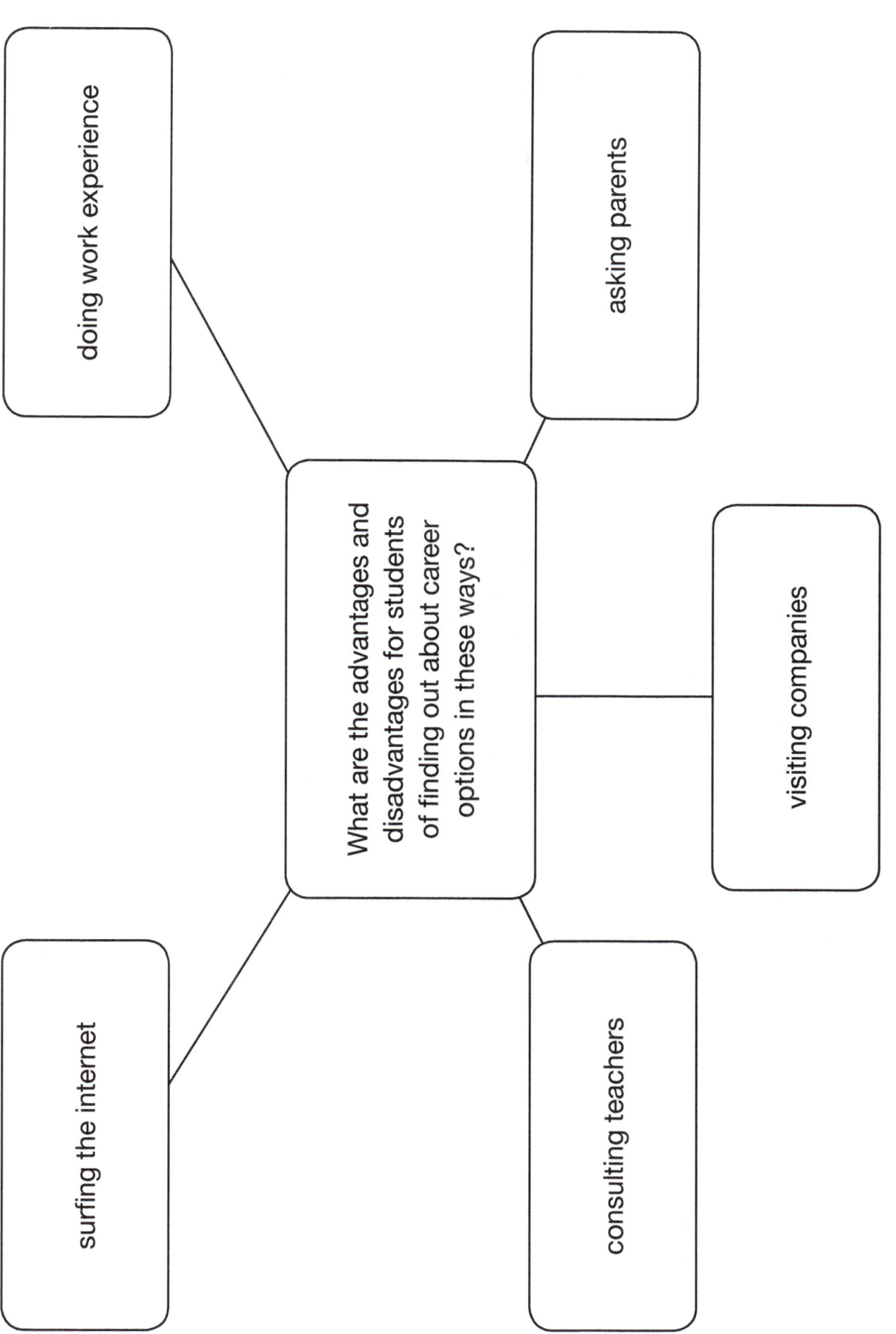

Part 2 Candidate B

- Why might the screens be important to the people?
- How difficult would it be for the people to manage without them?

Part 2 Candidate A

- Why might the celebration be special to the people?
- How memorable might it be?

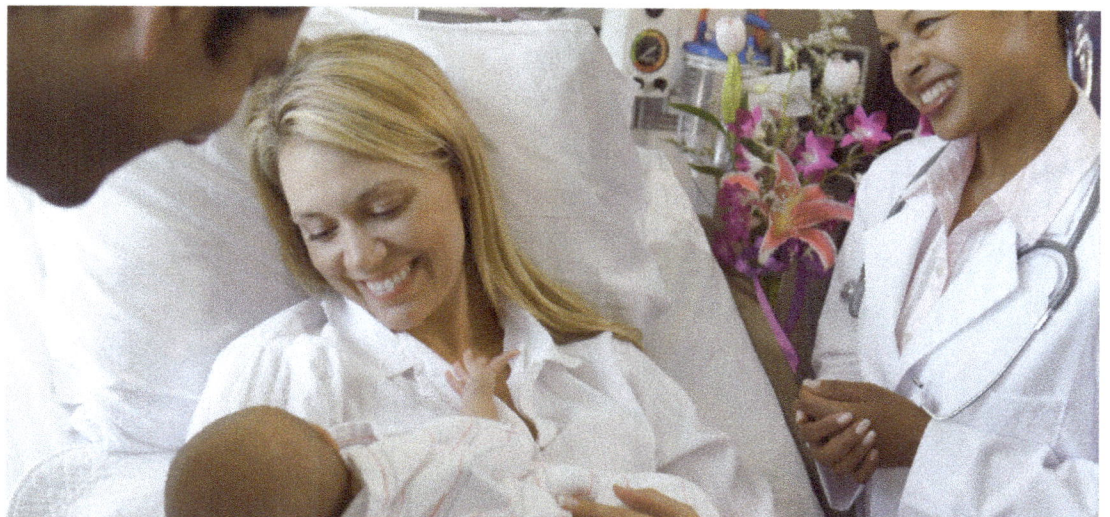

Part 2 Candidate B

- How easy might it be to play music in these situations?
- How important might it be for the musicians to practise regularly?

Part 3

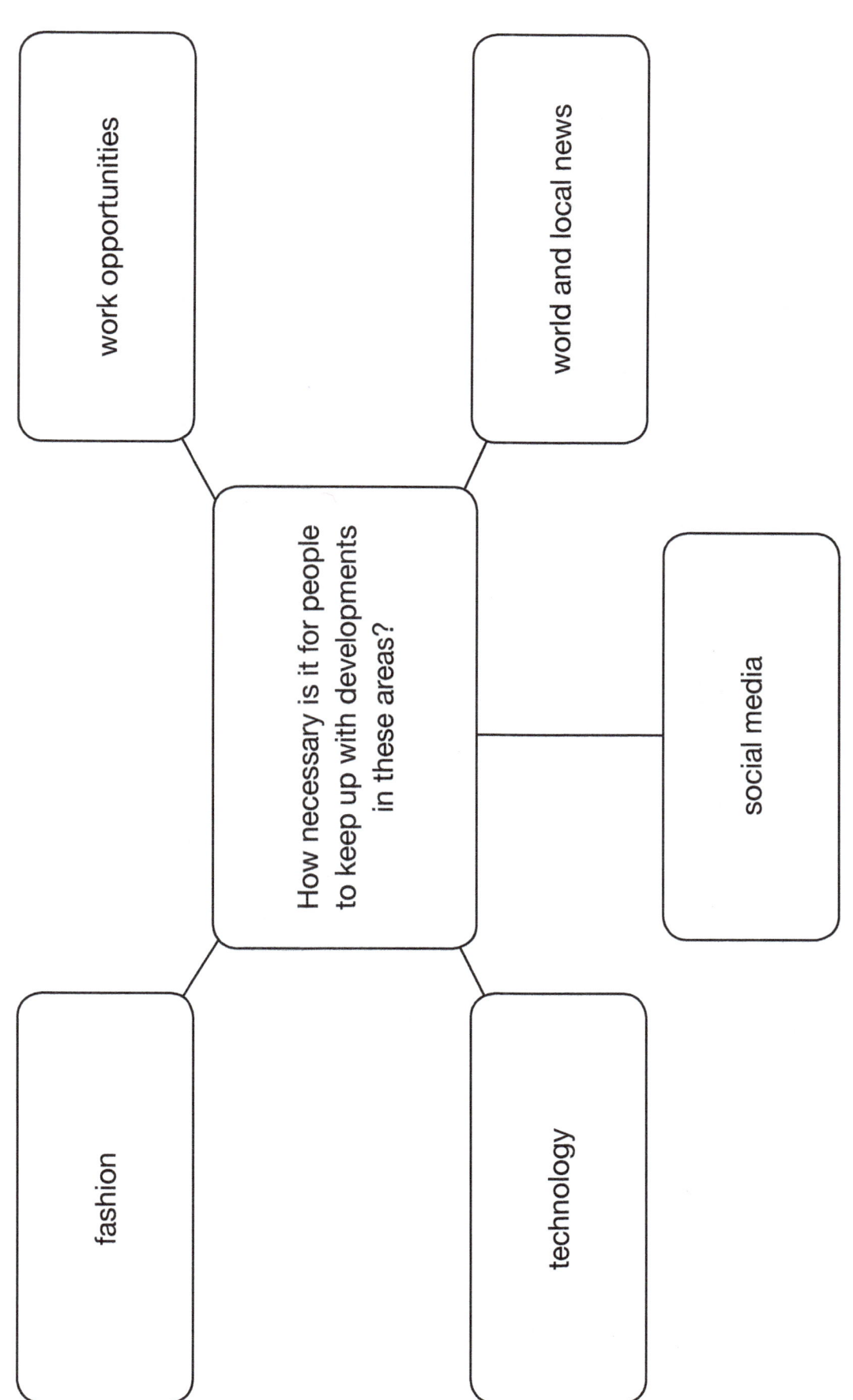

Part 2 Candidate A

- Why might the people be taking the photographs?
- How important might the photographs be to them?

Part 3

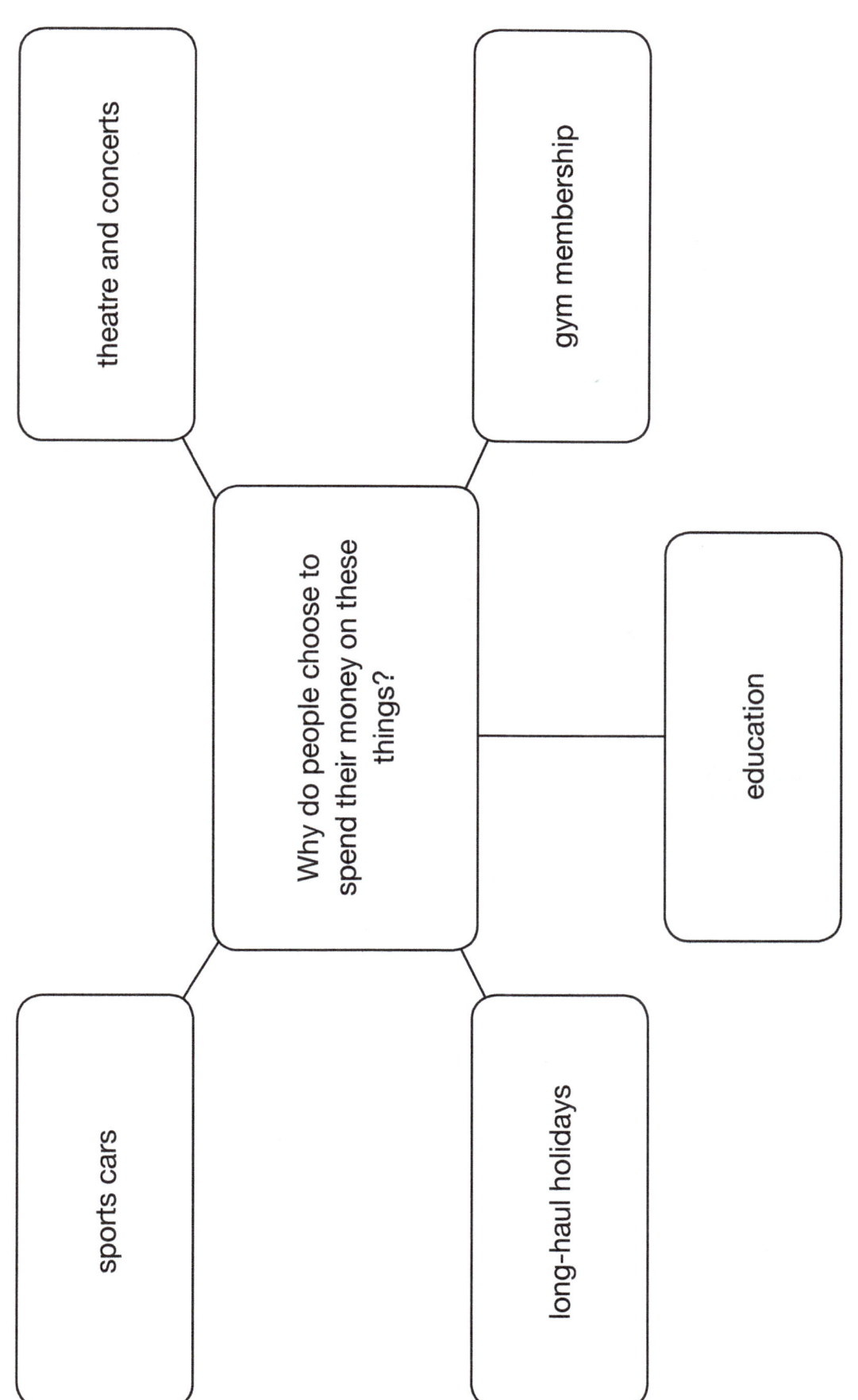

Part 2 Candidate B

- Why might the people have chosen to do this sport?
- How important might it be for them to do it regularly?

Part 2 Candidate A

- What might the people find hard about working in these situations?
- How easy might it be to deal with any problems?

Part 2 Candidate B

- What might people enjoy about taking part in activities like these?
- How difficult might it be to do them well?

Part 3

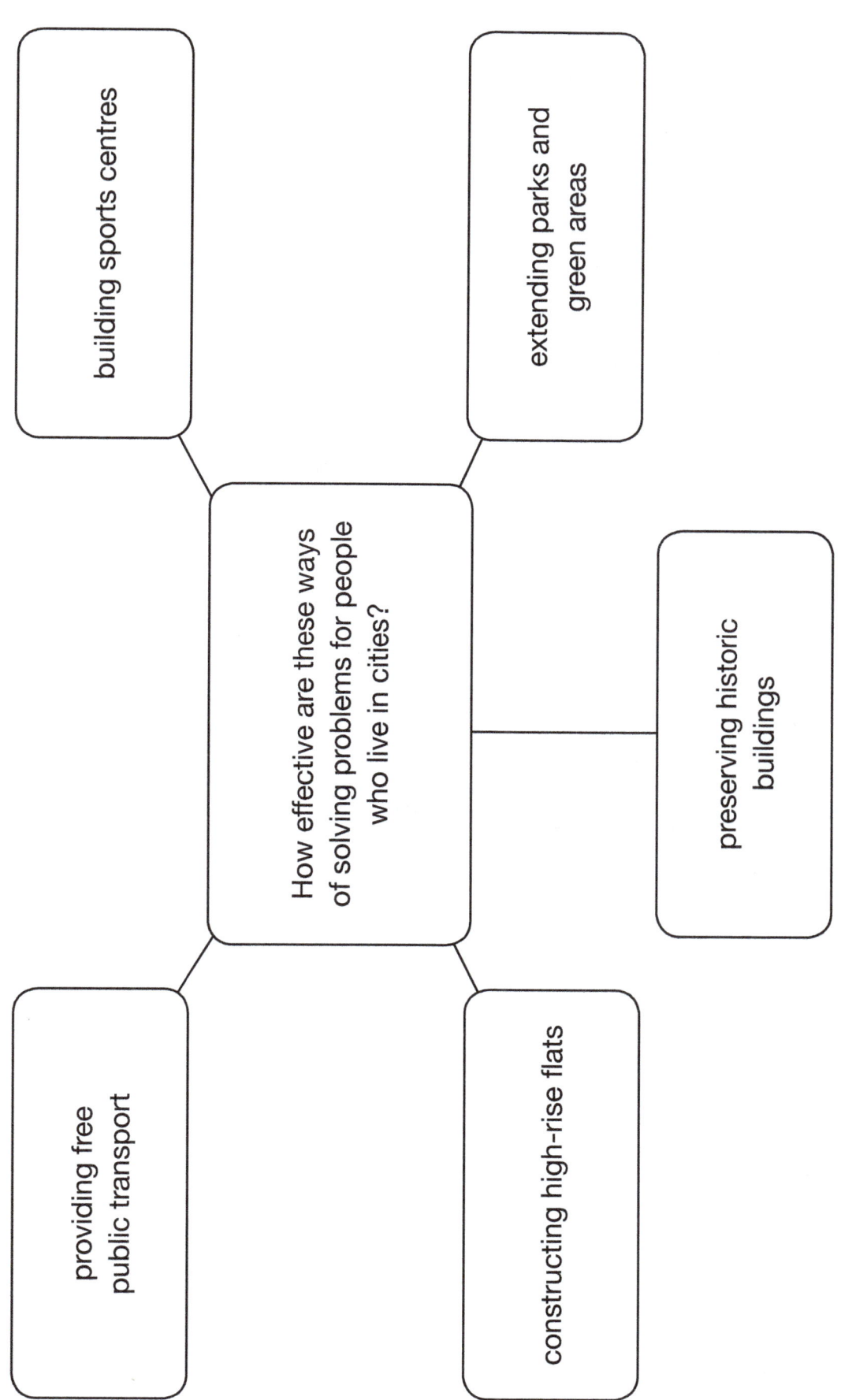

Part 2 Candidate A

- Why might the animals be important to the people?
- How might the people be feeling?

Part 3

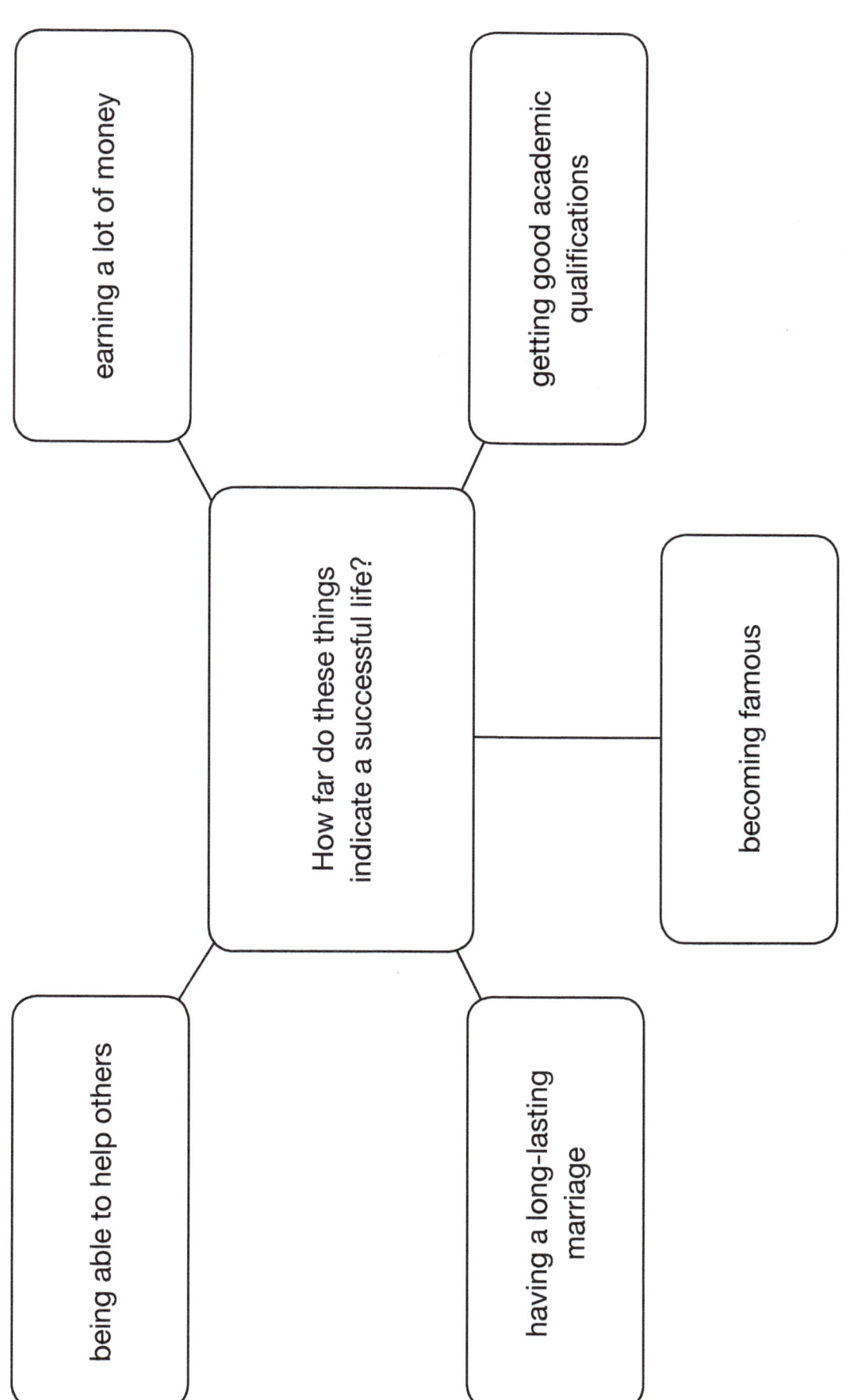

Part 2 Candidate B

- Why might the people have chosen to get around in these ways?
- Why might their journey be important to them?

Part 2 Candidate A

- Why might the people have chosen to study in these different places?
- How important might it be for them to be able to concentrate on their studies?

Part 2 Candidate B

- How easy might it be to entertain others in these situations?
- How important might it be to perform well?

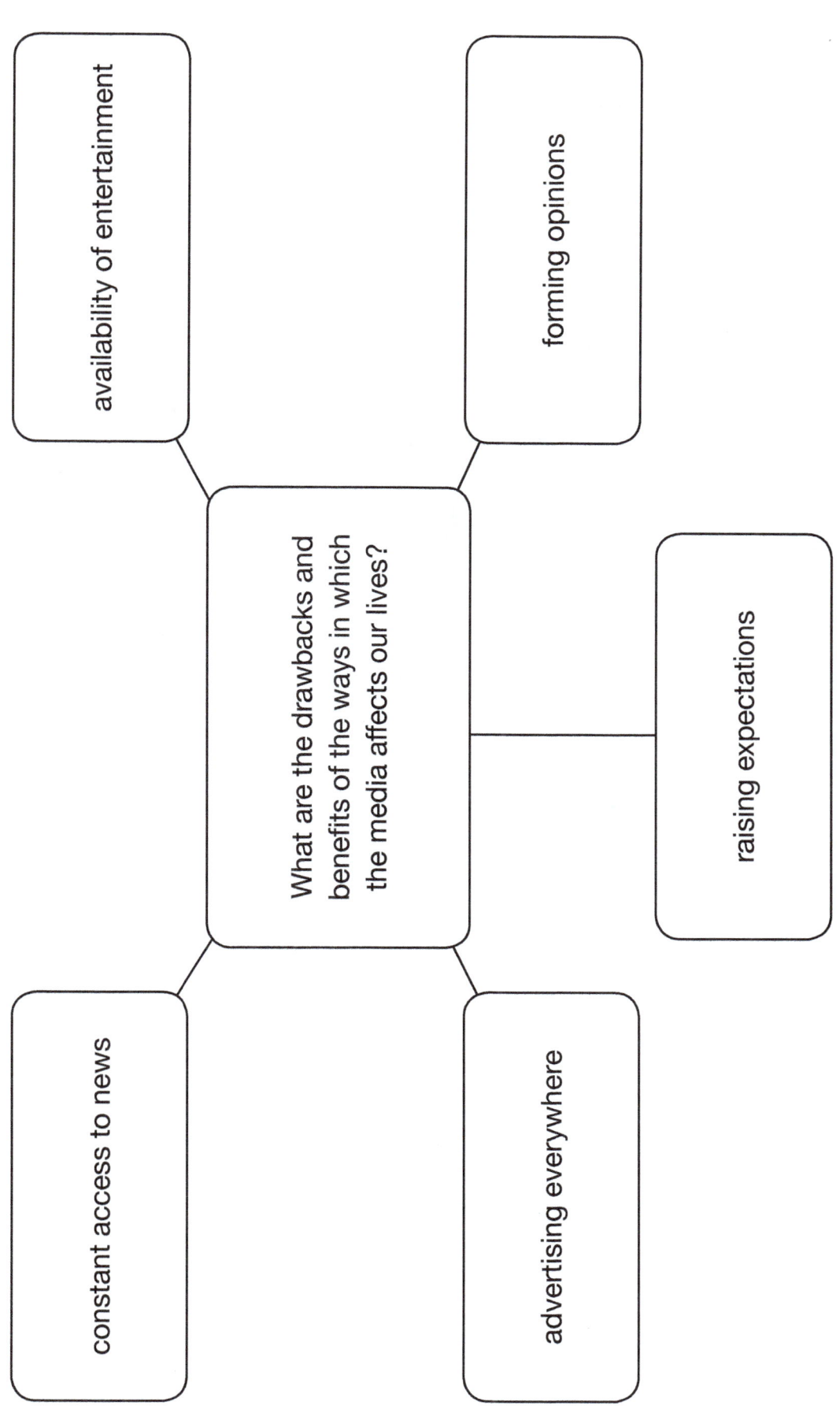

Part 2 Candidate A

- Why might the people need to take a short break?
- How might they feel if they didn't do this?

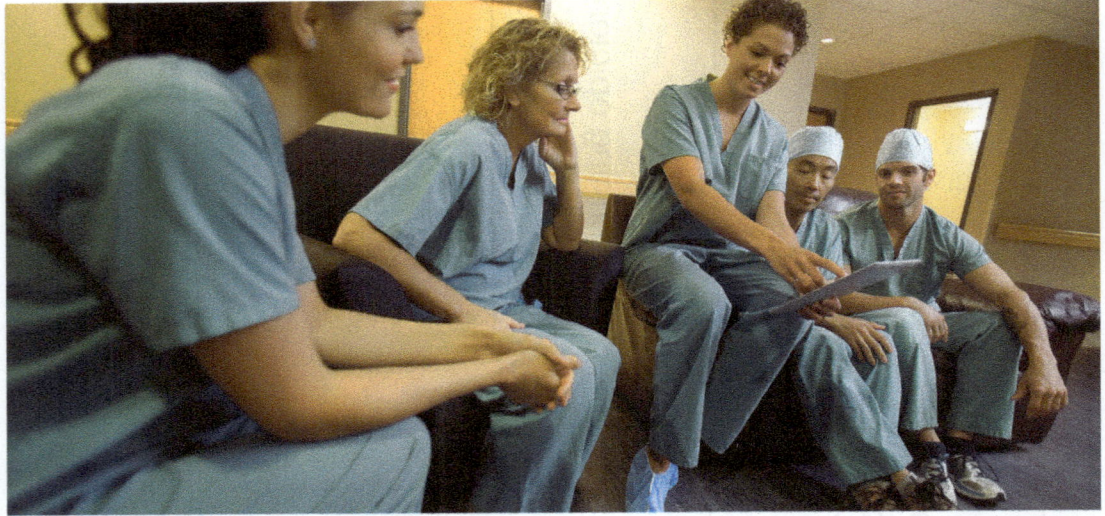

Part 3

How important is it for governments to spend public money on these things?

- setting up museums
- supporting theatres and art galleries
- funding medical research
- building motorways
- providing free pre-school education

Part 2 Candidate B

- Why might it be important for the people to do these things carefully?
- What might happen if they don't take great care?